Women Have Always Worked

A Historical Overview

Women Have Always Worked

A Historical Overview

Alice Kessler-Harris

HOFSTRA UNIVERSITY

The Feminist Press

NEW YORK

Photo Research by Flavia Rando

Distributed by The Talman Company, Inc., 150 Fifth Avenue, New York, NY 10011.

First edition, second printing

Library of Congress Cataloging-in-Publication Data

Kessler-Harris, Alice.
  Women have always worked.

  (Women's lives/women's work)
  Includes bibliographical references.
  Women—Employment—United States—History.
I. Title. II. Series.
HD6095.K45   331.4'0973   80-13400
ISBN 0-912670-67-3 (pbk.)

The findings and conclusions of this volume do not necessarily represent the views of the National Endowment for the Humanities.

Some of the material on pages 162–163 first appeared, in somewhat different form, in Alice Kessler-Harris, "American Women and the American Character: A Feminist Perspective," in *American Character and Culture in a Changing World*, ed. John A. Hague. Reprinted with permission of the publisher, Greenwood Press, a division of Congressional Information Service, Inc., Westport, Connecticut.

Table of Contents

Publisher's Acknowledgments

EARLY IN 1973, Mariam Chamberlain and Terry Saario of the Ford Foundation spent one day visiting The Feminist Press on the campus of the State University of New York, College at Old Westbury. They heard staff members describe the early history of The Feminist Press and its goal—to change the sexist education of girls and boys, women and men, through publishing and other projects. They also heard about those books and projects then in progress; they felt our sense of frustration about how little we were able to do directly for the classroom teacher. Advising us about funding, Terry Saario was provocative. "You need to think of yourselves," she said, "in the manner of language labs, testing and developing new texts for students and new instructional materials for teachers." Our "language" was feminism, our intent to provide alternatives to the sexist texts used in schools. The conception was, in fact, precisely the one on which the Press had been founded.

Out of the 1973 meeting came the idea for the *Women's Lives / Women's Work* project. This project, which would not officially begin for more than two years, has allowed us to extend the original concept of The Feminist Press to a broader audience.

We spent the years from 1973 to 1975 assessing the needs for a publication project, writing a major funding proposal, steering it through two foundations, negotiating with the Webster Division of McGraw-Hill, our co-publisher. We could not have begun this process without the advice and encouragement of Marilyn Levy of the Rockefeller Family Fund, from which we received a planning grant in 1973. For one year, Phyllis Arlow, Marj Britt, Merle Froschl, and Florence Howe surveyed the needs of teachers for books about women, reviewed the sexist bias of widely used history and literature texts, and interviewed editorial staffs of major educational publishers about their intentions to publish material on women. The research accumulated provided a strong case for the grant proposal first submitted to the Ford Foundation in the summer of 1974.

During the winter of 1974–75, Merle Froschl, Florence Howe, Corrine Lucido, and attorney Janice Goodman (for The Feminist Press) negotiated a co-publishing contract with McGraw-Hill. We could not have proceeded without the strong interest of John Rothermich of McGraw-Hill's Webster Division. Our co-publishing agreement gives control over editorial content and design to The Feminist Press; McGraw-Hill is responsible for distribution of the series to the high

school audience, while The Feminist Press is responsible for distribution to colleges, bookstores, libraries, and the general public.

In the summer of 1975, the final proposal—to produce for co-
publication a series of twelve supplementary books and their accom-
panying teaching guides—was funded by the Ford Foundation and the
Carnegie Corporation. Project officers Terry Saario and Vivien Stewart
were supportive throughout the life of the project. In 1978, The
Feminist Press received funds from the National Endowment for the
Humanities to help complete the project. Additional funds also were
received from the Edward W. Hazen Foundation and from the
Rockefeller Family Fund.

Once initial funding was obtained, The Feminist Press began its
search for additional staff to work on the project. The small nucleus of
existing staff working on the project was expanded as The Feminist
Press hired new employees. The *Women's Lives / Women's Work*
project staff ultimately included six people who remained for the
duration of the project: Sue Davidson, Merle Froschl, Florence Howe,
Elizabeth Phillips, Susan Trowbridge, and Alexandra Weinbaum. We
also wish to acknowledge the contributions of Dora Janeway Odarenko
and Michele Russell, who were on staff through 1977, and Shirley Frank
and Mary Mulrooney, on staff through 1978. Helen Schrader, a Feminist
Press staff member, participated on the project during its first year and
kept financial records and wrote financial reports throughout the
duration of the project.

The *Women's Lives / Women's Work* project staff adopted the
methods of work and the decision-making structure developed by The
Feminist Press staff as a whole. As a Press "work committee," the project
met weekly to make decisions, review progress, discuss problems. The
project staff refined the editorial direction of the project, conceptual-
ized and devised guidelines for the books and teaching guides, and
identified prospective authors. When proposals came in, the project
staff read and evaluated the submissions and made decisions regarding
them. Similarly, when manuscripts arrived, the project staff read and
commented on them. Project staff members took turns drafting mem-
oranda, reports, and other documents. And the design of the series grew
out of the discussions and the ideas generated at the project meetings.
The books, teaching guides, and other informational materials had the
advantage, at significant stages of development, of the committee's
collective direction. All major project policy decisions about such
matters as finance and personnel were made by The Feminist Press
Board at its monthly meetings.

Throughout the life of the project, The Feminist Press itself continued to function and grow. Individuals on staff who were not part of the *Women's Lives / Women's Work* project provided support and advice to the project: Jeanne Bracken, Brenda Carter, Ranice Crosby, Shirley Frank, Brett Harvey, Frances Kelley, Emily Lane, Carol Levin, Kam Murrin, Karen Raphael, Marilyn Rosenthal, Helen Schrader, Nancy Shea, Nivia Shearer, Anita Steinberg, Sharon Wigutoff, and Sophie Zimmerman.

The process of evaluation by teachers and students before final publication was as important as the process for developing ideas into books. To this end, we produced testing editions of the books. Field-testing networks were set up throughout the United States in a variety of schools—public, private, inner-city, small town, suburban, and rural—to reach as diverse a student population as possible. We field tested in the following cities, regions, and states: Boston, Massachusetts; Tampa, Florida; Greensboro, North Carolina; Tucson, Arizona; Los Angeles, California; Eugene, Oregon; Seattle, Washington; Shawnee Mission, Kansas; Martha's Vineyard, Massachusetts; New York City; Long Island; New Jersey; Rhode Island; Michigan; Minnesota. We also had an extensive network of educators—350 teachers across the country—who reviewed the books in the series, often using sections of books in classrooms. From teachers' comments, from student's questionnaires, and from tapes of teachers' discussions, we gained valuable information both for revising the books and for developing the teaching guides.

We would like to thank the following people with whom we consulted about *Women Have Always Worked: A Historical Overview.* Their thoughtful and detailed responses to the material were extremely helpful to us. Mildred Alpern, Spring Valley Senior High School, Spring Valley, New York; Mari Jo Buhle, American Civilization Department, Brown University; Allen F. Davis, Department of History, Temple University; Sarah Elbert, Department of History, SUNY Binghamton; Mary Lynn Hamilton, Cholla High School, Tucson, Arizona; Beth Millstein Kava, Adlai Stevenson High School, Bronx, New York; Natalie A. Naylor, New College, Hofstra University; Jan Rosenberg, Empire State College; Anne Firor Scott, Department of History, Duke University; Walter S. Smith, School of Education, The University of Kansas; Barbara Wertheimer, New York State School of Industrial and Labor Relations, Cornell University; Joanna Schneider Zangrando, American Studies Department, Skidmore College.

Three times during the life of the *Women's Lives / Women's Work* project, an Advisory Board composed of feminist educators and scholars met for a full day to discuss the books and teaching guides. The valuable criticisms and suggestions of the following people who participated in these meetings were essential to the project: Mildred Alpern, Rosalynn Baxandall, Peggy Brick, Ellen Cantarow, Elizabeth Ewen, Barbara Gates, Clarisse Gillcrist, Elaine Hedges, Nancy Hoffman, Susan Klaw, Alice Kessler-Harris, Roberta Kronberger, Merle Levine, Eleanor Newirth, Judith Oksner, Naomi Rosenthal, Judith Schwartz, Judy Scott, Carroll Smith-Rosenberg, Adria Steinberg, Barbara Sussman, Amy Swerdlow. We also want to express our gratitude to Shirley McCune and Nida Thomas, who acted in a general advisory capacity and made many useful suggestions; and to Kathryn Girard and Kathy Salisbury who helped to develop the teacher and student field-testing questionnaires.

One person in particular whom we wish to thank for her work on *Women Have Always Worked* is Flavia Rando for her exhaustive photo research and her unbounded enthusiasm for the job. Indeed, her research unearthed so many excellent photographs that it was with great difficulty that we limited ourselves to the ones that we finally selected for this volume.

Others whom we want to acknowledge are Ruth Adam for restoration of the historical photographs; Hedda Garza, who prepared the index; Angela Kardovich of McGraw-Hill for administrative assistance; and Miriam Weintraub and Les Glass of Weinglas Typography Company for the text composition.

The work of the many people mentioned in these acknowledgments has been invaluable to us. We would also like to thank all of you who read this book—because you helped to create the demand that made the *Women's Lives / Women's Work* project possible.

THE FEMINIST PRESS

Author's Acknowledgments

THIS BOOK GROWS OUT OF a larger study to which it is both parent and child. Many of the ideas presented here are the fruits of that other research and yet this book appears first—perhaps as an invitation to the next. Since I started working on the history of wage-earning women, in the early 1970s, I have received generous research aid and support from a variety of sources including the American Philosophical Society, The Rabinowitz Foundation, and the National Endowment for the Humanities. My grateful thanks to all of these as well as to the Radcliffe Institute which housed me for half a year, and to Hofstra University for the several leaves that enabled me to take advantage of the fellowships.

The manuscript benefited from the criticism of good friends and colleagues. Blanche Wiesen Cook, Amy Swerdlow, and Phyllis Vine read the manuscript through, providing trenchant criticism and numerous specific suggestions. Elizabeth Phillips at The Feminist Press has been a knowledgeable and versatile editor—full of inspiring enthusiasm. Bert Silverman's clear vision has encouraged me to see in this book, as in the many projects on which we have worked together, some of the connecting links to the struggle for social change.

I have dedicated this book to my daughter, Ilona, who shared in its creation and was its first reader.

ALICE KESSLER-HARRIS

Women Have Always Worked

A Historical Overview

For Ilona

ONE:
The Meaning of Work in Women's Lives

DOTHA BUSHNELL LIVED ON A CONNECTICUT FARM in the early 1800s, among the last of generations of American women who worked in households that produced all of the necessities of

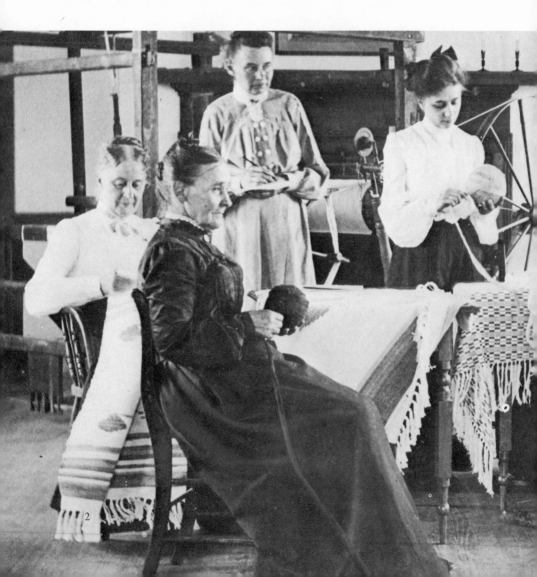

survival. Her son, Horace, lamenting the disappearing past, wept over the "frugal, faithful, pious housewife" who lived in an age when "the house was a factory on the farm; the farm a grower and producer for the house." All of a household's members were harnessed together "into the producing process, young, old, male and female, from the boy that rode the plough horse to the grandmother knitting under her spectacles."[1]

Nobody then or now could wonder if Dotha Bushnell worked. In preindustrial societies, nearly everybody worked, and almost nobody worked for wages. But with industrialization, the harness yoking household members together loosened. As produc-

tion began to move out of the household into factories, offices, and stores, those who got paid for the new jobs were clearly workers. At the same time, the kinds of work women did at home changed dramatically. The remaining tasks of the household, such as caring for children, food preparation, cleaning, and laundering, were not so clearly defined as work. In separating the job necessary to maintain the household from the job done for pay, the industrial revolution effected not only a shift in the tasks assigned to workers of either sex, but a shift in perceptions of what constituted work. Women who maintained the home and did not collect wages were no longer considered workers. Their home roles appeared as something other than work.

Sharp distinctions in male and female jobs contrast with the preindustrial period when both men and women did what could, in one sense, be called domestic work. As servants, slaves, or family members, their tasks revolved around the household that constituted the center of production. Among family members, women as well as men derived identity, self-esteem, and a sense of order from their household places. For slaves and servants, whose work lives centered in other people's families, household tasks were nevertheless the source of survival. For the most part, the core family and its extended members consumed the goods and food produced in this unit, trading what little there was left to make up for shortages.

There seems to have been a rhythm to the work performed in this preindustrial environment, in harmony with the seasons in the countryside and with family needs in both town and country. By the sixteenth century, much of Europe had what we would now call an unemployment problem: too many workers and too few jobs. To feed, clothe, and shelter the population at minimal levels required fewer workers than the numbers of people available. As a result, work was spread out. The evidence suggests that traditional role divisions, which assigned to women internal household tasks and care of gardens, dairies, and domestic animals, allowed men a good deal more freedom than their wives. Men, more than women, benefited from a growing labor surplus. Women's tasks tended to be less seasonal and more regular. Over the span of a year, men had less onerous regular responsibility.[2]

The transition from this relatively self-sufficient domestic economy to dependence on trade took hundreds of years and developed at different speeds in different areas. The first inroads occurred when the commercial revolution of the thirteenth century created a market for manufactured goods and encouraged craftsmen and their families to concentrate their energies on producing for cash. These artisan families, who had previously made and sold their own products, began to produce for merchants who bought in bulk and sold to distant places. In these family industries, women, who were excluded from formal apprenticeships, could nevertheless become skilled in crafts. And they were partners in every other sense of the word. In most places the law acknowledged a wife's right to the business if a husband died. The garden plot still produced food supplies, and wives and widows supervised and trained young unmarried women to perform household work. If labor within these artisan families seemed relatively balanced, it was far from idyllic. Work within the household, in the shop, and on the farm was always hard. Poor crop yields or sickness could bring even comfortable households to the edge of starvation.

As trade developed in the seventeenth and eighteenth centuries, however, a subtle change came over family industry. Merchants, who had at first been content to take what was available and sell it, soon began to demand products made to their own specifications. Instead of gathering the products of local artisans, they "put out" their own orders to cottages throughout the countryside. Workers lost control over what they made. They still retained control over their time. People who worked in their own cottages would not be rushed. They did more or less work as other tasks called, and sometimes they wasted materials. As orders increased, however, merchants required faster and more reliable production. Effective supervision of workers could be obtained only if the labor force were concentrated in one place. And toward the end of the eighteenth century, the development of steam-powered machinery required a labor force able to move where the machines were, adding urgency to the demand for a factory work force.

Slowly and painfully the laboring poor were persuaded to give up their own loosely jointed and self-imposed definitions of work. In sixteenth- and seventeenth-century England, land that had been held in common for generations, as well as some that had traditionally been leased by families, was taken over by large landowners for their own use. This process, called enclosure, meant that some farm families were forcibly ejected while others no longer had common pasture. Ultimately, they could not survive on the land. Driving men, women, and children from farms made them available for work in towns. But they were reluctant workers. Employers could persuade them to show up for work regularly only by holding back wages or tying them to contracts that ran for as long as twenty-one years. Sometimes employers beat inattentive workers, especially children. Frequently the state passed laws to help employers create a reliable work force. In England and France, harsh laws against vagrancy forced people to take jobs against their own inclinations. Those who would not submit might be branded or jailed and later deported to colonies in far-off places.

Work in the Colonies

As in the old world, workers in the colonies did not easily submit to the idea of working by someone else's rhythms. In early Virginia this proved to be a special problem. Historian Edmund Morgan describes how Virginia's first colonists starved rather than bow to what they saw as the harsh discipline of the Virginia Company. They chose to work only six to eight hours a day, spending the rest of their time "bowling in the streets." These work patterns, reminiscent of English habits, lasted until the Virginia Company imposed a quasi-military regime.[3]

The northern colonists required less pressure. Because their land was not owned by an outside company, and because many of them had come to America for common religious reasons, most early New Englanders shared an incentive to work. Puritan religion equated hard work with godliness, and salvation with the visible demonstration of God's bounty, so New England colonists drove themselves to accumulate earthly goods. Material reality enforced religious injunction. Unlike Virginia settlers, the Plymouth and Massachusetts Bay colonists had no company in England to call on for supplies in their early years. Throughout the colonial period, they suffered from severe labor shortages which only their own efforts could offset. And lacking appropriate raw materials to trade with England, they relied far more on homespun yarn and hand-woven fabrics than the southern colonies, which quickly developed tobacco and hemp as resources for trading.

Since all the colonies relied more or less on household production, women's work was necessary and recognized. Colonies initially gave plots of land to settlers and their families. In Maryland and South Carolina, women who were heads of families got allotments equal to those of men. For a few brief years, Salem gave "maid lots" to unmarried women, and Pennsylvania granted them seventy-five acres each. But opposition to unmarried women holding land developed early. Historian Julia Spruill cites a bill passed by the Maryland Assembly in 1634, and then vetoed by the proprietor. The legislators would have decreed of an unmarried woman that "unless she marry within seven years after land shall fall to hir, she must either dispose away of hir land, or else she shall forfeit it to the next of kinne, and if she have but one Mannor, whereas she cannot alienate it, it is gonne unless she git a husband."[4]

Without land, women had no source of sustenance except employment or marriage. Fearful that such women would become dependent, the colonists quickly passed laws that bound people who had no visible means of support out to work. Women, it was thought, were especially prone to vice and immorality, and colonies as different as Massachusetts and Virginia paid special attention to those women who, having no homes in the conventional sense, might fall into bad habits.[5] Harsh economic considerations undoubtedly motivated the colonists. Since pregnancy was a likely result of immorality, and there were few jobs for unwed mothers with small children, such women were likely to need public relief. Afraid of the potential costs, communities were especially careful to refuse female transients permission to settle.[6]

The assumption that women could and should participate in the production of necessary goods persisted well into the eighteenth century, and in many areas even later. When the colonists became concerned about having adequate supplies of cloth and yarn in the revolutionary period, they appealed to women's patriotic sentiments to increase supplies. George Washington wrote to his friend General Lafayette that he would not force the introduction of manufactures to the prejudice of agriculture. But, he added, "I conceive much might be done in the way of women, children, and others without taking one really necessary hand from tilling the earth."[7]

In contrast to much of Europe, where the imposition of work discipline required breaking old habits, in America colonists had already accepted an emphasis on work and industry before the onset of industrialization. This eased the task of disciplining a labor force for factory work. Where the Puritans had seen material prosperity as a demonstration of God's grace, the people of the early nineteenth century saw it as a manifestation of self-control and right living. Religious injunction was thus supplemented by new ideas of individualism, which made each person accountable for his or her success. Egalitarian notions that had emerged in the revolutionary period enhanced these ideas. Theoretically, at least, success was now plausible for even the lowliest people, slaves, people of color, and women excepted. Benjamin Franklin, who saw wealth as its own reward, urged people to depend "chiefly on two words: industry and frugality; that is waste neither time nor money, but make the best of both."[8]

The Success Ethic

The emphasis on individual achievement inherent in an ideology that glorified success threatened to eliminate entirely the older notion that individual well-being was intimately bound to the well-being of the community. It was one thing to spin and weave for the public good—and to reap material rewards incidentally. It was quite another to work for others for the sake of their profit alone. By the time Andrew Jackson became president of the United States in 1829, it seemed clear that those workers who could afford to own a small shop or a piece of land, quickly rejected the routinization of the factory for a promised independence.

White American workers had some advantages over workers in older European societies. Relatively cheap, available land encouraged free workers to save money and move west. Employers were willing to let them go since a steady influx of immigrants replaced them. For these workers, the promise of independence and of upward mobility provided incentives to work hard. Yet these incentives did not always produce the kind of work force employers felt they needed.

To integrate native- and foreign-born peasants, farmers, skilled artisans, and day laborers into a changing society required, as historian Herbert Gutman has pointed out, a continual process of acculturation. Each generation had to be taught to shed its old patterns and habits and to adopt those required of steady routine workers.[9] To accomplish this, factory owners quickly resorted to old-country methods of discipline. Factories might be located in idyllic country settings, like Dover, New Hampshire, or North Andover, Massachusetts, but their morning and evening bells called people to work with the same insistence as those in any of Manchester, England's satanic mills. Fines and locked gates forced workers to adhere to the factory rules. To obtain jobs, workers frequently had to agree to serve at least one year or to forfeit two weeks of wages. Employers ruthlessly blacklisted those of whom they disapproved. Bonuses went to those who showed up regularly for work and did not drink. Six-day work weeks protected workers against the "temptations" of leisure, and manufacturers even tried to regulate how time was spent on the seventh day.

The most extreme coercion occurred within slavery. In the South, employers occasionally offered slaves the chance to
(text continued on page 12)

The Working Lives of Women in the U.S.

Women have always worked—in their homes and the homes of others, in fields, factories, shops, stores, and offices. The kind of work done has varied for women of different classes, races, ethnic groups, and geographical locations. And the nature of women's work has changed over time with urbanization and industrialization. What remains the same is that the ways in which women have worked involve a constant tension between two areas of women's lives: the home and the marketplace. Left: woman hauling a basket of cotton, Savannah, Georgia, late nineteenth century. Right: women working in a cannery, early twentieth century.

purchase their freedom by dint of learning a skilled craft. Men might become blacksmiths or carpenters, while women might learn fancy sewing or hire themselves out as cooks. More often, however, slaves got no reward for hard work, and extreme punishment for slacking off. The cruelty of many masters measures the resistance slaves demonstrated to their lives of toiling for others.

Free white Americans believed strongly enough in the work ethic and in the possibilities for success to create the institutional support systems needed to sustain them. By the 1830s, a number of states funded public elementary school systems. Working men's groups, as well as social reformers, advocated free schools on the grounds that they would help educate the populace to the high levels demanded by democratic government. Designed to teach basic literacy and elementary arithmetic, the schools also instilled regular habits, cleanliness, and attention to detail: all mechanisms for creating an efficient work force. By and large, instruction was by drill and by rote. Most public schools soon aimed to reproduce the situation children would face at work. Teachers enforced discipline by shame, and children, according to historian Michael Katz, were "programmed from an early age to compete with one another." By teaching competition and individualism, the schools helped ensure that children of working people "would not grow up to form a cohesive and threatening class force."[10]

Like schools, Protestant churches exalted success. For them it offered evidence of morality. In the words of one famous preacher, "No man in this land suffers from poverty unless it be more than his fault—unless it be his *sin*."[11] Some clerics justified low wages and poverty as necessary to strengthen character. They offered solace in the form of a better world to come.[12] As late as 1877, Henry Ward Beecher, perhaps the nation's best-known preacher, earned the undying enmity of the labor movement when he thundered his opposition to the railroad strikes of that year. Workers should bear their poverty more nobly, he argued. After all, "is not a dollar a day enough to buy bread with? Water costs nothing, and a man who cannot live on bread is not fit to live."[13] The legal system confirmed what ideology left undone. It criminalized "conspiracies" among workers who formed trade unions to improve their bargaining power and threatened jail for the debtor and starvation for those who did not succeed in the competitive struggle.

Few people escaped the harsh constraints of working life. Increasingly, expectations of long days and minimal wages drove out notions of humane work. Time after work, or leisure time, became the pleasurable moments in individual lives. Competition replaced notions of cooperative work. As the nineteenth century moved into the twentieth, technology reduced the work process to ever simpler levels. Wage work became increasingly more monotonous and alienating. The home remained the last refuge of all that was nurturing and caring.

These changes were justified in terms of the success ethic. If hard work was a way of "making it," it could be tolerated, even glorified. But success for men was not success for women. Sociologist Alice Rossi has captured the dilemma succinctly. From the perspective of a white male, she argues, "American society in 1820 was an open vista of opportunity: by dint of hard work he could hope to improve his position in society; if he did not succeed in one locality, he could move on to another, carrying his skills with him...." At least in theory, the hardworking white male, with the emotional and financial support of a family, had access to newly available jobs in medicine, law, and the professions. Whether or not many actually succeeded in these terms was less important than the myth that they could.

But for women, black or white, the notion that success could be achieved by individual effort had the opposite effect. For black women, it perpetuated an endless cycle of hard work, with economic and social discrimination preventing the promised rewards from materializing. At the same time, white women, excluded from paid work and with the production of necessities within the home diminishing by the year, were, in Rossi's words, "effectively cut off from participation in the significant work of their society."[14] How then was woman's labor to be rewarded if not by tangible demonstrations of her productive capacity? To those women for whom industrialization brought an end to the unity of work and home, women's virtue came to be measured in terms of her supportive functions in the home.

Woman's Separate Sphere

A thicket of biological and social arguments emerged over a period of several decades to justify woman's exclusion from paid labor and her relegation to what Americans were pleased to call her "separate sphere." While black women, still largely slave and largely rural, continued to toil ceaselessly, urbanized white women faced a new set of demands. Appeals to women's natural inferiority, her small brain, her lack of physical stamina, and her delicate sensibilities were used to justify the social roles women were forced to adopt as the industrial revolution spread. The rhetoric hid what should have been apparent by the nineteenth century. Depriving women of paid labor had created a financially dependent strata. Dependence in turn spawned a series of behavioral characteristics, personality traits, and cultural expectations that were reinforced by persistent discrimination against women who sought paid labor.

The arguments for a "separate sphere" drew strength from the changing needs of the paid work force. If urban working men did not require wives to labor with them on the land, they did require supportive environments to help them maintain the competitive pace. A dependent wife not only confirmed a man's ability to make money, but also offered the clean socks, prepared meals, and disciplined children that hard-working husbands had no time to participate in creating. By the nineteenth century, economic expectations of urban middle-class women had shrunk. Instead of producing goods in the home, middle-class women would spend their time engaged in caring for children and ministering to the emotional needs of family members.

This "separate sphere" must have been attractive to many women. For women who needed to work for pay, the kinds of jobs available were of the most menial sort. Ivy Pinchbeck, a historian of eighteenth-century England, has pointed out that the industrial revolution offered for the first time to free women from the burden of two jobs.[15] Instead of bearing responsibility for producing some of the goods to be used in the home and for running the household, women could devote their attention to the latter task alone. From that perspective, and in a time when the task of maintaining a household included a wide variety of chores, the possibility of not having to engage in paid employ- ment must have seemed appealing indeed.

Women who maintained households and did not work for wages retained a pocket of freedom. Barren as it sometimes was, home was a refuge from harsh factory discipline or its alterna- tive: the relentless pressure of paid domestic service. In one of those curious moral trade-offs, women became the guardians of moral values at home—enabling men to assume competitive roles. Women's task was to preserve the humane, nurturing, collective, and caring aspects of an individualistic and competi- tive world. Women who stayed in their homes worked. Yet they were, and have remained in diminishing numbers, among the few people with the possibility of working at their own pace, by their own lights. The kind of work for which they were trained left them relatively free of the hierarchical, competitive, aggres- sive, and status-ridden world for which men were socialized. Work done for self and family at least retained the possibility of being creative, individualized, and nonalienating. Although it was often hard and could become rote, work in one's own home offered a freedom that toiling in someone else's house or factory never did.

The costs of this trade-off were not small, just different for women than for men. The home itself reproduced some of the dominant-subordinate relationships to which the work force subjected people. "True" women were expected, in historian Barbara Welter's definition, to be pious, pure, submissive, and domestic.[16] Since the "lady" was defined in reference to her father or husband, dependence was assured. Societal institutions confirmed these ideas. Laws deprived a woman of her property upon marriage, gave a husband claim to all of a wife's wages, and turned over the children to him should she commit any impropriety or ask for a divorce. A "lady's" family was to be the only sphere in which she could shine, her only occupation. Schools included her only peripherally in the lower grades and generally excluded her from advanced academic study. Those women forced by necessity into paid employment found themselves relegated to the most menial and poorest paid tasks: a confirmation of the injunction that they ought not to be in the work force at all.

In the absence of an identity derived from wage work, woman's identity was grounded in her home role. Especially for middle-class women, status, even self-esteem, came through men, giving truth to the old saying: man does, woman is. While many, perhaps most, women derived gratification from husbands and children, the evidence indicates that substantial numbers of women hungered for greater self-determination and resented their inability to achieve in their own right. Margaret Fuller wrote in 1843, "Many women are considering within themselves what they need that they have not, and what they can have if they find they need it."[17] Yet lacking opportunities for economic self-sufficiency, only a few exceptional women could achieve success by male standards. Some of the most successful, like Sarah Josepha Hale, a widow who edited a widely read magazine called *Godey's Lady's Book*, and the author Sarah Payson Willis Parton (better known as Fanny Fern), earned their livings by advocating a female reticence they did not themselves practice.

Bread and Roses

For most ordinary women, the unappealing nature of wage work made confinement to the hearth an attractive alternative. Increasing specialization of labor in the late nineteenth and early twentieth centuries produced barren work experiences for most men and women. Women in the paid labor force retained sufficient connection with expectations of freedom and cooperation to demand not merely adequate wages, but some joy in life. Marching down the streets of Lawrence, Massachusetts, in 1912, striking women carried banners that proclaimed, "We want bread and roses too." Poet James Oppenheimer, watching the parade, immortalized the words in a poem that went on to say, "hearts starve as well as bodies."[18]

The particular expectations women brought into the labor force, stemming from their different experiences, have in some ways been used to keep women in subservient positions. As one nineteenth-century mill manager wrote, "Women are not captious and do not clan as the men do, against the overseers."[19] But the same sensitivities and expectations enable women to make demands for more humane working conditions where men might not. The ways in which women have worked involve a constant tension between the two areas of women's lives: the home and the marketplace. This tension is the crux of our understanding of women's working lives.

To describe women's household work as merely auxiliary to paid work in the labor force, or to talk about some women as "not working" ignores both the value of housework in sustaining the labor force, and its relationship to the wage-working lives of women. Wage work and household work are two sides of the same coin. Scratch one side deeply enough and the other will be blemished.

Classifying what women did at home and in the marketplace as either "nonwork" or auxiliary work became a way of avoiding a confrontation with how women worked. What they did at home, because it was unpaid, could easily be shunted aside. And when they began to move into industry in large numbers, their low pay and menial conditions were justified by considering their wage work as mere preparation for home roles. Defining women's work this way was useful. It confirmed women's status as subordinate or auxiliary to that of men. The household was forced to rely on male income, since women's wages were insufficient to sustain households. And, women were less likely to seek wage work as jobs were not attractive anyway. These conditions also ensured a continuing supply of cheap labor at times of labor shortage.

Though many women were drawn into the labor force for a while, most managed to drift in and out of it in response to family needs. Up until 1900, less than 20 percent of all women over fourteen were in the paid labor force at any one time. Black women, who rarely had the option of working only at home, engaged in paid labor at about three times the rate of even immigrant women. The numbers of native-born white women earning wages did not begin to increase dramatically until after World War I. Up until the 1960s, though many women worked for wages at some point in their lives, especially as young adults, the normal expectation was for women to be unpaid housewives. With some major exceptions for black women and recent immigrants, paid labor did not constitute the focus of most women's lives. Almost all women could hope that they would be free of wage work for a while.

That is no longer the case. Since World War II, changes in technology and the structure of the work force have multiplied the likelihood that women will work outside their families. The argument that family needs dictate that a woman stay home has broken down, and in 1979 more than half of all adult women in America worked for wages. This new reality has raised questions about household tasks. Who should do them and under what circumstances? Do family needs still require that women take less demanding jobs than their husbands? Is it possible to alter all jobs so that both partners can share economic responsibility as well as family work? Can families alter to accommodate the changing personal needs of their members?

The issues that emerge from these questions are all around us: equal pay for equal work, affirmative action, day care centers, new kinds of families. Much of the debate on these issues is related to outdated notions of work for women.

This book will define work in the manner of a commission appointed by the United States Department of Health, Education and Welfare in 1973. Work, the commission wrote in its final report, is "an activity that produces something of value for other people."[20] Whether the product is then sold or distributed at no cost never figures in the definition, and later in its report, the commission explicitly includes housework. The report also cites some familiar examples of the rewards of work. Work is a source of identity, helping all of us to locate ourselves within the society and to feel a sense of value as contributing members. It enhances self-esteem, offering a sense of mastery over self and society. Work provides economic security and, a frequent correlate, family stability. It can help create a sense of order and structure. Within its sphere, people decide where and how to live. Without work, rootlessness threatens and, as in periods of economic depression, vagrancy replaces community building.

The kind of work women have done over the past two hundred years has created sensibilities that differ from those of men. Can women now leave their own sphere without giving up what is best in their lives? Is it possible for women simultaneously to join the work force on an equal basis with men and to alter it in ways that accord with their own sensibilities?

TWO:
Household Labor

NOTHING EMBODIES A GREATER CHANGE in the way women have
worked than the transformation of their household tasks. The
colonial goodwife would hardly recognize her twentieth-century
counterpart—even if she were to be reincarnated on one of the
few remaining family farms. And an urban woman of the 1970s
would shudder with horror at the tasks laid before the colonial

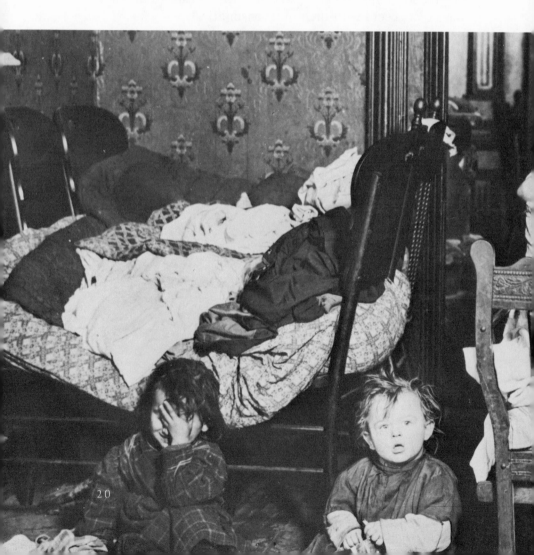

dame. Yet as much as their specific tasks have changed, an unbroken thread binds the roles of these two women together. A continuous line connects women's work in the seventeenth-century colonies with their work in urban and computerized twentieth-century America. The changing context in which women have worked disguises the similarities. But society's expectations of women have remained virtually the same down to, if not including, the present day. An interesting question is whether, at last, those expectations are changing.

The transition in women's work at home can be viewed from a variety of perspectives. The structure and organization of household work has been altered. The way people experience

that work has changed dramatically. And, the transition from rural to urban society, and from scarcity to relative affluence, has worked its changes. Each of these perspectives casts a different light on work done in the home.

The Colonial Household

From all three perspectives, change begins in the realities of a preindustrial economy. Its demands determined the way most women worked. Until at least the middle of the eighteenth century, there was little market for the exchange of goods, and households operated as units of production centered around the self-supporting farm or the artisan's shop. Food, clothing, and furnishings emerged from the efforts of every household member. Most families produced nearly all of their household goods. Very few families produced for the "market" or for sale, although some of their grain surplus might purchase such things as rum, coffee, tea, salt, sugar, and potatoes. And some surplus might be necessary to pay for the services of the occasional lawyer or minister, or for the journeymen, tradespeople, and artisans who provided articles difficult to make. Some households made their own boots, while others relied on itinerant shoemakers. Rudimentary carpentry, soap and candle making, spinning, weaving, sewing, and knitting, were the province of every household.[1]

A surprising amount of flexibility existed in the tasks people did. Although women's efforts usually focused on work in and around the home, it was not unusual for a woman to pitch hay at harvest time or to plow in the spring. Similarly, men spent twilight hours alongside their wives at the loom, and through the eighteenth century, boys, like girls, were trained to spin and weave. A division of labor by sex, though common, was not rigid. The amount of cooperation among household members that was required to produce a piece of linen cloth, for example, is revealed in the following paragraph taken from Alice Morse Earle's *Colonial Dames and Goodwives*. First the flax was pulled and spread in rows to dry.

This work could be done by boys. Then men whipped or threshed or rippled out all the seed to use for meal; afterwards the flax stalks were allowed to lie for some time in water.... Then came work for strong men, to break the flax on the ponderous flaxbreak...and to swingle it with a swingle knife, which was somewhat like a wooden dagger.... It was then hetchelled or combed or hackled by the housewife, and thus the rough tow was gotten out, when it was straightened and made ready for the spruce distaff round which it was finally wrapped.... The thread was then spun on a "little wheel." It was thought that to spin two double skeins of linen, or four double skeins of tow, or to weave six yards of linen, was a good day's work. For a week's work a girl received fifty cents and her "keep." She thus got less than a cent and a half a yard for weaving.[2]

Some chores were seasonal: linen making; candle dipping; preserving of fruits, meats, and vegetables each happened once a year. Other tasks were more frequent. Clothes might be washed in huge steaming tubs once each month. Soap making occurred several times a year. When sickness interfered, the housewife collected herbs, prepared medicines, and nursed the ill. Yet the daily chores never disappeared. Cows had to be milked and eggs collected at the henhouse. The fire had to be lit and tended. Bread was baked several times each week and meal preparation took endless hours. Spinning and weaving cloth and sewing garments were early evening activities performed in the relative quiet of a day mostly done.

Patterns varied regionally. In the South, for example, a white woman blessed with a milder climate and more fertile soil than her northern counterpart spent less of her time spinning and sewing clothing. For food, she probably relied more heavily on pigs, which, fed from slops or allowed to forage, provided adequate meat the year round. Yet these advantages were offset by the longer growing season, which meant more outdoor toil if the kitchen garden were to yield its abundant supply of potatoes and vegetables. The southern frontier family tended to be more isolated than the community-oriented New England family. Circumstances required strength and self-reliance: women frequently handled rifles, hunted, trapped, and defended themselves against predatory creatures. It was all part of the job.

Women of wealth were spared some of these tasks. They depended on other women—slaves and servants—to do them. It is perhaps a measure of the need for self-sufficiency that wealthy women took pride in their housework. Julia Spruill, historian of the colonial South, described one notable woman who made "minced pies, cheesecakes, tarts and little biskits. . . ." which she distributed daily.[3] A South Carolinian, herself a notable intellectual, proudly wrote to her new son-in-law, "I'm glad your little wife looks well to the ways of the household."[4] For these women, daily tasks normally involved giving instructions rather than drudgery. Yet their responsibilities were immense. Like the wife in a New York manor house, the plantation wife provided food for a large household and its frequent visitors. She ran the dairy, supervised the gardens, managed and instructed servants, ordered supplies, and planned menus. She cared for the health of the family and sometimes of numerous servants and slaves. And she attended to all the social necessities as well. More often than not, she was called upon to make decisions about the planting and harvesting of crops as well as about their storage and sale. In her husband's absence, and sometimes in his presence, she took over the barter and exchange of crops for household supplies, earning a well-deserved reputation as an astute tradeswoman. If we do not need to feel sympathy for this privileged member of society, we should at least acknowledge her work as the business manager of a complex establishment.

The daily labor of this establishment—all of the menial work required to keep it going—was performed by slaves. At first, the status of a slave was uncertain. Most early colonists treated slaves like indentured servants, freeing them after several years of labor. But within twenty years after the first shipload of black people was sold at Jamestown in 1619, colonies began binding persons of color—and their children—for their lifetimes. Blacks thus became more valuable than whites as servants. The absence of a legal contract enabled masters to use them virtually at will.

None of the informal protections that applied to white women applied to black women. No qualms of conscience prevented white owners from putting black women to work in the fields, to plant, plow, dig, and harvest alongside their men. In fact, before 1660 both Virginia and Maryland explicitly acknowledged the

work of black women in the fields by taxing them in just the same
way they taxed male field hands. Yet slave women were not
exempt from household work. They laundered, nursed, cleaned,
and cooked in the big house, and they also had all those
obligations for other slaves and their own families. As one ex-
slave put it somewhat later, they worked "from can to can't from
the time they could see until the time they couldn't."[5] Despite
rampant sexual exploitation and frequent family separation,
slave families struggled to maintain a sense of family existence.

Northern householders relied less on slaves and more on *North*
servants, male and female. Servitude took on a variety of forms.
Common to most of them was the characteristic of being
"bound." A person gave herself or himself over, or was given over,
to service for a specified number of years, which could range up
to a lifetime. Binding a servant out carried reciprocal obligations.
In return for labor, the master or mistress agreed to a range of
things from merely sustaining life to teaching servants how to
read, write, and cipher, and sometimes teaching them a trade. In
the case of a young woman apprenticed to housework, the
master or mistress might be obliged to teach the arts of spinning
and weaving. These conditions were not always honored, and
servants often resorted to the courts to force their masters to
adhere to the contract. Both men and women were bound out.
Probably about two fifths of the servants (and one third of the
slaves) were female through the colonial period. How people
were bound out made all the difference in the kind of work
demanded and the treatment accorded.

Indentured servants, who signed contracts before emigrating
from Europe, normally bound themselves out for five to seven
years in return for passage to the New World and food, clothing,
and shelter during service. If they fulfilled their terms, most
indentured servants got "freedom dues"—generally an outfit of
clothing, a small payment, or a farm animal. Redemptioners
differed from indentured servants in that they did not normally
negotiate their own service, but were "sold" on arrival by a ship's
captain for the cost of passage. As a result, they had no
bargaining power or choice as to length or kind of service. Less
fortunate than indentured servants, they were infinitely better
off than slaves because their length of service, working condi-

tions, and compensation were protected by contract and enforced by stringent colonial laws. In practice a female indentured servant or redemptioner normally performed the tasks of the female householder. She worked in the dairy, the kitchen garden, and within the home. Often she spun yarn and wove cloth with the mistress. Rarely was she expected to do field work, and then usually only in cases of dire need.

Indentured servitude carried no stigma. In many respects, and especially in the eighteenth century, it was indistinguishable from the binding out of young girls by parents who either could not support them, or who believed they would be better trained in the household arts by strangers. Nor was the condition of the indentured servant distinguishable from that of the woman, who, having no family, bound herself out as a means of insuring herself a home. These various forms of binding out continued, until after the Revolution, to provide homes and training for large numbers of women. In turn, these women provided services without which households could not have functioned.

Yet a servant was a servant. Women were forbidden to marry during their term of service. Pregnancy, which threatened to deprive masters of some of their labor, was punishable by extending the term of the indenture—sometimes by three to four years. It was not unknown for unscrupulous householders to make their servants pregnant and then demand extra time from them. Colonial laws notwithstanding, householders often tried to coerce more than a fair day's work out of their help. Some of the complaints of servants have come down to us. Listen, for example, to the "trappan'd maiden" who claimed she had been sent to Virginia against her will and who asked her readers to "Give ear unto a Maid, that lately was betrayed...."

Since that I first came to this Land of Fame
Which is called Virginny, O,
The Axe and the Hoe have wrought my overthrow,
When that I was weary, weary, weary, O.

Her calendar of complaints included the following: When her lady "sits at meat, then I have none to eat.... The cloathes that I brought in, they are worn very thin.... Instead of Beds of Ease, to lye down when I please.... Upon a bed of straw, I lye down

full of woe.... Instead of drinking Beer, I drink the water
clear.... I have played my part both at Plow and Cart...Billets
from the Wood, upon my back they load."[6] Bad as her lot was, she
did not seem to approach the desperation of poor Elizabeth
Spriggs whose father banished her from his sight for some
unknown offense. "What we unfortunat English People suffer
here," she wrote,

is beyond the probility of you in England to Conceive, let it suffice
that I one of the unhappy Number, and toiling almost Day and Night,
and very often in the Horses druggery, with only this comfort that you
Bitch you do not halfe enough, and then tied up and whipp'd to that
Degree that you'd not serve an Annimal, scarce anything but Indian
Corn and Salt to eat and that even begrudged nay many Negroes are
better used, almost naked no shoes nor stockings to wear, and the
comfort after slaving dureing Masters pleasure, what rest we can get is
to rap ourselves up in a Blanket and ly upon the Ground, this is the
deplorable condition your poor Betty endures, and now I beg if you have
any Bowels of Compassion left show it by sending me some Relief,
Clothing is the principal thing wanting.[7]

Not all women servants took harsh treatment readily. Many
ran away from their masters; some stole food, clothing, and
money in order to do so. Despite liberal rewards, catching a
servant was no easy task, for she blended easily in the population
of any urban area. Women who were caught often paid dearly.
Courts added anywhere from four to eight days of extra toil for
each day she was gone to the indenture of a servant. And she was
also assessed the expense of her capture.

Until the end of the eighteenth century, well over 90 percent
of the population lived on the land. Yet in growing commercial
towns, skilled crafts became the basis of the household economy. In the homes of the blacksmith, the shoemaker, the
silversmith and pewterer, the tailor and milliner, the shop
normally occupied one part of a dwelling establishment—
sometimes the front or basement. The dwelling also housed the
apprentices and journeymen who worked in the shop, any other
servants, and all family members. Female servants might do
some of the laundering, cooking, and cleaning for the family and

apprentices, but female family members were also expected to do household work. In addition, they, like male family members and apprentices, were engaged in the craft work of the household. Excluded from guilds, women could not usually become apprentices and develop their own craft. But many a father taught his daughter everything she needed to know to run a printshop or even a smithy. Numerous widows, who had carried the burdens of family businesses while their husbands were living, easily continued the work after the men died.

What of women without property? Or single women? What of women whose husbands were ne'er-do-wells, or sickly? What work could they do? Their options were few. The most fortunate set themselves up in trade, acting as brokers, or running small shops. It was not unusual for women with husbands to run inns, or to brew and sell ale and beer. With a little training a woman could become a milliner, a mantua maker, or a seamstress. She might knit stockings at home to sell in the town or to a factor—a merchant who resold them to shops in distant parts. With slightly more training, women ran dame schools for young children. And they were universally in charge of community health: midwiving babies, wet-nursing the young, nursing the sick, and caring for the elderly.

But in the end, few women could survive comfortably unless they had households to sustain them. Those who did not have homes of their own most often bound themselves out as servants. So marginal was the condition of women with children and without husbands that towns routinely denied them permission to settle for fear that they would become public charges. To ensure that transients could claim no legal right to support, towns notified or "warned" them to get out after a specified number of days. Women's sex was no protection against being warned off. One historian notes that equal numbers of women and men were warned off.[8] The lucky few found work spinning and weaving in public almshouses.

The most essential tasks of women centered around childbearing and child rearing. Because most of the demographic data is based on surviving children, figures vary as to the number of births a typical woman might have had. In a society where large numbers of children did not survive infancy, the available statistics severely underestimate the amount of time women spent bearing children. Yet the scanty data that exists reveals that reproduction was no easy task. A typical woman might bear a child approximately every two years for a period of twenty years. If her first child came when she was about twenty-two and her last when she was in her mid-forties, she would bear ten or eleven children. Of these, perhaps eight would survive into adolescence. If the last child left home at fifteen, the mother would have spent thirty-five years having and rearing children.

Ann Bradstreet, America's first poet, herself an original settler and daughter of one of Plymouth's early governors, had eight children. She was lucky, for all eight survived into adulthood. Yet she writes of the deaths of some of her tiny grandchildren in poems which reflect her loss. There was her "dear grandchild Elizabeth Bradstreet, who deceased August, 1665. being a year and a half old," and Anne Bradstreet, her namesake, "who deceased June 20. 1669. being three years and seven Moneths old," and poor Simon Bradstreet, "Who dyed on 16. Novemb. 1669. being but a moneth, and one day old."[9]

Though bearing children was uniquely women's task, child rearing after infancy was not. Parents jointly assumed responsibility for training their children, sharing the tasks of education and discipline. Mothers normally taught girls household tasks, and fathers trained boys in the way of husbandry. The young people they trained included some who were not their own. For since the household was a place of production, efficient use of labor encouraged parents to send their own children away from home and to take others in. The child so placed, often at the age of nine or ten, acted as a servant or apprentice in the home to which she or he went. Twelve-year-old Elizabeth Nevinson went from her parents' house to the home of the Hammond family in 1688. Lawrence Hammond noted in his diary that "Elizabeth shall dwell with my wife as a servant six yeares, to be taught, instructed, and provided for as shalbe meet, and that she shall not depart from our family during the said time without my wives consent."[10] Elizabeth's parents probably expected that apprenticing their daughter in this way would save her from overly fond indulgence. Such young women had no protection from the toil that a colonial household demanded of all its members, although a network of custom and law protected them from physical abuse.

Elizabeth perhaps found in the Hammond household a structure very much like the one she had left. An ordinary, reasonably comfortable house in New England around that year, where husband and wife were in their mid-thirties, probably included a range of children from a suckling baby up to an adolescent. The oldest two or three might already have been bound out, especially if they were boys. Mothers relied on the ten- and eleven-year-olds for help. In such a household, there might well have been an aging parent and perhaps an unmarried sister to help with the work. A little more prosperity allowed the family to hire a servant girl—a practice that increased in the eighteenth century as old notions of discipline broke down and parents became more reluctant to trade their daughters. Hired help surely existed for the man of the house. Further south, slaves were substituted for servants in affluent houses, and the household tended to become larger.

Colonial women who were not slaves or servants must have had some sense of their own importance. Where there was no separation between production and consumption, where husband and wife and offspring were engaged in a common enterprise, where the work, however hard, was clearly a part of the common purpose of the household, women could feel little of what sociologists now call role conflict. Ideas about what women were supposed to do corresponded closely with what in fact they did in their daily lives. Good performance not only produced tangible satisfaction in well-fed and prosperous households, but it garnered societal praise as well. Yet even before the war for independence, this had begun to change, and a visible narrowing of women's roles was underway.

The Household Transformed

No single factor altered the work of women at home, nor did their lives alter all at once. At least two separate processes contributed to the way household tasks began to change in the colonial period. Both began in the northern colonies and worked their way south and west. The first emerged from the household itself, out of a natural desire to ease the harsh burdens of survival. The second was imposed by British mercantile policy. Both are intertwined with ongoing urbanization and incipient industrialization.

As long as the family farm was relatively self-sufficient, neither a woman's daily work nor the demands made of her changed substantially. Self-sufficiency did not, however, mean no exchange with other families. Quite early on, most towns built themselves grist mills which relieved families of the chore of grinding their own grain. Families exchanged work on large tasks, like building houses, sewing quilts, and boiling down molasses from sugar cane. More frequently, they exchanged commodities. A family short of candles borrowed them from another, sending in return some soap, eggs, or whatever was surplus. Barter extended to the general store. Women traded such items as woven cloth, hats, yarn, and bunting for cash equivalents against items purchased. And sometimes they traded what they had produced for the services that would ease their tasks.

Take, for example, the carding of wool. When a sheep had been sheared, and the burrs and twigs picked from the mounds of fleece, the mass had to be combed or carded to ready it for spinning. The task was long and arduous. And when professional carders advertised their willingness to do it in no time at all, women welcomed having the task done for them. Carders advertised that they would comb specified amounts of wool, cleaned and dyed, in return for a pound of the finished product. The temptation to trade for services provided an incentive to produce a surplus. And soon commercial factors roamed the countryside urging women to spin their yarn for trade, often in return for a number of yards of woven cloth.

Such trade remained in the province of small home manufacturers longer than might have been expected. This was a consequence of the way British regulations enhanced the importance of what women produced in the colonial economy. British mercantile policy assumed that the colonies would produce raw materials to feed the incipient manufacturing industries of the mother country or would provide food or tobacco. But it quickly became apparent that except in the South, where tobacco, pitch, tar, and later sugar and cotton, became cash crops, the colonies could neither pay for British goods in adequate quantities of raw materials or food, nor rely on England for all their needs.

Beginning as early as 1640, when the British civil war temporarily cut off supplies of goods, the separate colonies began a policy of encouraging women to spin and weave from raw wool, hemp, and flax. That year Massachusetts ordered a systematic investigation of the capacity for spinning in the colony and urged that both boys and girls be taught to spin. To encourage greater production, Massachusetts also agreed to pay weavers a bonus of 25 percent over the value of woven cloth. Later laws were more specific to women, providing, for example, that "all hands not necessarily employed on other occasions, as woemen, girles, and boyes, shall, and hereby are, enjoyned to spin according to their skill and abilitie...."[11] The law demanded that each family with one spinner produce three pounds of linen, cotton, or wool a week for thirty weeks a year. Pressure on women to spin and weave waxed and waned as the economic situation of the various colonies changed. But no one ever doubted that when necessity commanded, women should take up their wheels.

Mercantile regulation became more severe in the late seventeenth and into the eighteenth century. The colonists could not trade with each other in certain manufactured goods. In 1699, for example, the British prohibited the colonists from loading any manufactured article of wool onto a horse, cart, or carriage, thus making trade, at least on paper, impossible. As the Revolution approached, exporting technology, information, and machinery from England to the colonies became illegal.

Mercantile laws were never stringently enforced. Yet insofar as they inhibited the development of factories of any size, they encouraged the perpetuation of home manufacture. This, of course, was not women's task alone. Shoes, pewter, and iron products came from the shops of male artisans. But women carried the burden of making cloth, clothing, hats, and food.

Colonial laws and regulations compensated for the absence of English goods by offering bonuses to women who fulfilled these tasks.

The pressures of mercantilism and the colonial resistance to British restrictions mounted in the last half of the eighteenth century. Finally the unpopular Stamp Acts of 1764 led the colonists to retaliate with a series of "non-importation" agreements that made buying domestic goods a patriotic act. In Lynn, Massachusetts, shoemakers multiplied their production perhaps ten times over between 1760 and 1768. The demand for homespun rose, encouraging merchants to speed production by a variety of methods. Public spinning bees invited ladies to take up their looms on the Boston Common. Home manufacture mounted dramatically as merchants offered higher prices for spun yarn. The market for knitted goods expanded.[12]

Women who had spun and knitted largely for family use now found themselves capable of commanding steady, if small, incomes from their goods. But the pressure that encouraged women to work at home soon had a contrary effect. The movement toward political independence that led women to develop their household skills also fostered the creation of technology to increase the quantity of manufactured goods. In the resulting competition between household manufactures and factory-made goods, the household quickly lost ground.

Rolla Milton Tryon, historian of household manufacturers, identifies three phases of the manufacturing process between the close of the revolutionary period in 1783 and the end of the Napoleonic wars in 1815. First women rushed to buy the imported goods that they had been deprived of in the seven-year-long war for independence. Then, patriotism and expense pushed them back to household products. And finally, the new nation's surge toward industrial independence led to rapid technological development and an expansion of small shops and factories. This all but eliminated the incentive for household manufactures to continue.

By 1800, women in some locations could choose to pay for one or more of a variety of processes and to discontinue them at home. Fulling and dying mills readied woolen cloth for sewing. Carding shops demonstrated their ability to produce more spun yarn from a pound of wool than homemade carding. Flax might be broken and linen bleached at central locations. Itinerant weavers, and factors who advertised their willingness to spin for a share of the product, serviced large numbers of communities. Women who could afford to pay for these goods had little temptation to perpetuate onerous work. Steam-powered machinery could make better quality cloth and finer yarn than the housewife, and at prices that encouraged her to stop spinning and weaving altogether.

Some indication of how dramatically household tasks shifted comes from figures on household production in the early years of the nineteenth century. In New York State, for example, in 1825, each household still produced nearly nine yards of fabric per household member. Within ten years, the figure had dropped to little more than four yards. By 1855, New York State's households averaged only a quarter of a yard of fabric per person. Household spinning and weaving had become dying arts.[13]

These figures reflect the impact of the new market economy. As the household carried less of the burden of production, the need for female labor in it diminished. Although no one would argue a one-to-one relationship between the function of the household and its composition, by the early nineteenth century the birth rate had begun to decline, and households were shrinking visibly in size. In towns like Andover, Massachusetts, demographer Philip Greven found an absolute decline in population.[14] By 1850, the average white native-born woman would bear only five children—half the number her great grandmother had borne. In poorer households, older daughters could now more easily be spared from family work, sometimes to go off to labor in factories for a while before returning home. Ancillary members of the household became scarcer. Unmarried sisters could make places for themselves in towns, perhaps teaching school. Throughout the first half of the nineteenth century, the size of the household continued to contract as the work done in it gravitated toward commercial enterprises.

In the North, servants and farm help were no longer as available as they had been, and the character of demands made on them began to change. While affluent households North and South might maintain a number of servants or slaves, increas-

ingly in the nineteenth century, households relied on a single
"maid of all work" whose lot visibly deteriorated as she shoul-
dered the work that in the past might have been done by a
laundress, a cook, and a number of maids. And, much more than
in the colonial period, the paid labor of a servant was dis-
tinguished from the work of the "lady."

The Affluent Housewife

Most women continued to work hard in the home throughout
the nineteenth century. For women who were slaves, work
continued as usual to involve both field work and household
labor. Rural women and poor women, rural and urban, did all
their own household labor or worked alongside any servants
they had. For well-off urban women, however, the nature—
though not necessarily the amount—of their household work
changed significantly. The "lady" North and South set aside her
spinning wheel. For increasing numbers of middle-class women,
the tasks of bearing and raising children and of making the
household a "comfortable" place for family members expanded to
replace earlier productive duties. And so, throughout the nineteenth century, the difference between the kind of work
performed by middle-class and affluent women and that done by
poor and working-class women increased dramatically.

The new role of the middle-class wife involved sustaining the
values and life of a household where the husband no longer
worked at home, side by side with his wife, but went out to the
world. Such a woman was expected to be cheerful and warm,
responsible for the smooth and orderly running of a household
which would offer her husband the services he needed to sustain
his work life. Her central tasks, in historian Nancy Cott's words,
involved "service to others and the diffusion of happiness in the
family."[15] But these were only the means to fulfilling her
ordained role. In her hands lay the guardianship of those moral
values that would redeem the crass materialism of an exploding
commercial culture. As men paid increasing attention to earning
(text continued on page 38)

Taking Care of Family Needs

Throughout American history, women have done unpaid domestic work. They have cleaned their homes, cared for children, planted and harvested family gardens, cooked and served meals, and generally ministered to the emotional needs of family members. In some cases, they have done this in addition to their paid work, which has included taking in boarders, doing piecework at home, and leaving the home to work for wages. Frequently, their unpaid domestic labor has not been considered "work." Left: canning fruit in the kitchen, c. 1900. Top right: scrubbing the front steps. Bottom right: woman with children in a collard patch, 1902.

moral role of women in home

a living, women continued to mold the family in a way that would do it credit before God. On a daily level, this translated into a variety of specific tasks ranging from supervising and training servants to performing those acts of charity that had earlier been the community's collective responsibility. Making social calls, teaching Sunday School, these were all signs that a woman took her calling seriously.

No greater demonstration of piety existed than the effort women put into rearing their children. Fathers who increasingly took jobs outside the home left mothers to raise children in ways that were consistent with godly values and yet not inconsistent with the future need to earn a living in a godless and competitive world. This apparent contradiction was exacerbated in the Jacksonian period by spreading notions of egalitarianism that forced even well-born men to struggle to advance themselves. The ethos of individualism placed the burden of failure squarely on the shoulders of the competitor. The contradiction was reconciled in the person of the mother, who was to inculcate both faith and self-discipline. Prevailing ideas held that the future of the republic rested on her efforts at continuing regeneration of moral purpose.

The clearest expression of these ideas occurred first among the prosperous and growing urban middle class. In what historian Bernard Wishy calls a reappraisal of family life that took place after 1830, motherhood rose to new heights of importance, and children became the focus of womanly activity. Mothers were asked to give up wealth, frivolity, and fashion in order to prepare themselves for a great calling. "The mother was the obvious source of everything that would save or damn the child; the historical and spiritual destiny of America lay in her hands."[16] Simultaneously, the woman became a "lady." Meek and passive, modest and silent, women were expected to submerge their wills into those of their husbands and fathers. Piety, purity, and submissiveness became the ideals. Women could fulfill these precepts only within the home. As one imperious writer pointed out, "the dictates of nature are plain and imperative on this subject, and the injunctions given in Scripture, no less explicit."[17]

Sanctifying the household in this way did not lessen the

amount of physical labor performed in it. It did relegate that
continuing hard work to second place, transforming the public
image of the household by the 1820s and 1830s from a place
where productive labor was performed to one whose main goals
were the preservation of virtue and morality. Volumes of
literature written in this period contributed to glorifying
women's spiritual and emotional roles in the household by
telling women how they were expected to live. This prescriptive
literature was for many years interpreted by historians as a
description of how women actually lived. Recently, however,
some historians have begun to read the diaries and letters of
nineteenth-century women. They have uncovered a different
picture of the middle-class housewife's life. Many of the "well-
run" homes of the pre-Civil War period seem to have been the
dwellings of overworked women. Short of household help,
without modern conveniences, and frequently pregnant, these
women complained bitterly of their harsh existences. Martha
Coffin Wright concluded a list of instructions in a letter to her
sister in 1847 with the following comment: "I know one thing—
let me once get an independent fortune, and I will gladly impart
all the valuable information I possess on such subjects, but as to
practising—I believe I have done it my share."[18] Even the
southern lady, with all her slaves and a house in town, worked.
Anne Firor Scott describes the life of a Vicksburg railway
official's wife who "sewed continually and was so burdened with
household cares that she felt guilty about sitting in the parlor
talking to guests unless she had sewing in her hands. She, too,
planted her own garden, took up carpets in spring, cooked and
washed, and cared for children, despite the fact that she was
never without household slaves."[19]

Catharine Beecher's *Treatise on Domestic Economy* has to be
seen within the context of the real work that most women did in
their homes. Published in 1841, the book suggested ways in
which women could rearrange their household tasks to lighten
their work loads. Recognizing that running a household was a
complex affair that required preparation and training, Beecher
set out to provide a manual to instruct women in everything
from the correct design of a kitchen to appropriate household
manners. In the years between 1841 and 1869, Beecher pioneered

the principles of efficient housewifery. She collaborated with her sister, Harriet Beecher Stowe, on a second edition of the book, published in 1869 with the title *The American Woman's Home.* This volume indicated how times had changed and offered an indication of things to come. It consisted of thirty-eight chapters that, together, constituted a cyclopedic compendium on such topics as house design and decoration; ventilation; heating; health care; nutrition and cooking; exercise; cleanliness; manners; household economy; care of infants, servants and the sick; social duties; and toilet construction.

The kitchen, center of the household, was to be organized on the principles of a ship's galley. Needed items were to be close at hand, well organized, labeled clearly, and in their proper places. The manual aspired "to elevate both the honor and the remuneration of all the employments that sustain the many difficult and sacred duties of the family state, and thus to render each department of women's true profession as much desired and respected as are the most honored professions of men."[20]

Like its predecessor, the *Treatise on Domestic Economy, The American Woman's Home* tacitly acknowledged that production for household use was no longer to be a woman's major function. It recognized that the housewife's job required knowledge and organization and, at the same time, it implicitly picked up the core of America's unique brand of individualism. By introducing a scientific element into housewifery, the Beechers offered to raise the status of woman's household work from the lowly position to which it threatened to tumble when its productive functions diminished. The Beechers sparked a movement, located at first in land-grant colleges and women's institutions, to train women in the domestic arts. The new home economics programs encouraged women to earn college degrees without threatening contemporary sensibilities about women's place.

Developing women's talents, freeing them from the worst aspects of household drudgery, opened the possibility that women might have other vocations. Some began to wonder whether domesticity ought to be women's highest calling. Women like Melusina Fay Peirce tried to find ways of getting women out of the kitchen altogether. Peirce founded the

Cambridge Cooperative Society in 1869 to organize services for households. A cooperative store, a laundry, and a bakery came out of its efforts. At the same time, she urged, but did not succeed in having built, kitchenless apartments with central house-keeping facilities. Marie Stevens Howland and Alice Constance Austin tried to adapt the egalitarian ideals of communal life to eliminate private domestic work entirely.[21] These women drew sketches of their prototype communities. No building ever took place.

For the vast majority of women, architecture, reflecting society's vision of family life, limited the possibilities of collective domestic work. Most women were bounded by the ideology of the time and the four walls of their family space. What they did within those four walls would change, however, with the introduction of new energy sources. In the mid-nineteenth century, cheap gas was brought into some house-holds. Toward the end of the century, electricity began to replace wood and coal in affluent homes. Gas and electricity offered the potential for changing housewifery. For those who could afford them, clean-burning fuels reduced the chopping and the carry-ing, eliminated much household soot and dirt, and produced instant heat and light. Late in the century, better-off families benefited from running water in the home. This replaced the well and the street pump from which water had been universally drawn and carried by hand, sometimes up several flights of stairs. And, finally, after the turn of the century, the oil- or gas-fired furnace made hot and cold running water plausible for all but the poorest homes. Individual houses with abundant energy and water provided the incentive to develop the small power motor at the end of the nineteenth century. This motor made electric-ally driven machinery a reasonable alternative to household work processes long performed by hand.

Changes in washing facilities offer an example of how quickly a middle-class woman's life could change. When one needed to draw water, chop wood to heat it, scrub each item by hand, rinse in clear water, and then clean the ashes after, it was little wonder that those who could afford to often employed laundresses. With both housewife and laundress working, laundry took a full day. Such rudimentary washing machines as existed before the advent of home electricity required steam heat and huge facilities. They were so cumbersome that they led Catharine Beecher to suggest neighborhood laundries where women could send the family wash. Even in the late nineteenth century, hand-cranked washing machine wringers and boilers were as close as the average household came to mechanical help with laundry. The invention of the small electric power motor in 1889, and its rapid adaptation to household uses, initiated the technology that made possible electrically powered "automatic" washing machines—reducing laundry for the middle class to a task that, by the 1920s, could be done in a morning of housecleaning.[22] Transforming technology did not mean eliminating household work. The wash once done by two women, or sent out of the home altogether, was now done by one alone.

Cook stoves, vacuum cleaners, and refrigerators also changed the nature of women's work. New equipment could eliminate the daily marketing trip, cleaning could be accomplished more rapidly, and meal preparation consumed less and less time. To these technological developments, the factory contributed its share. Processed and canned foods, invented for Civil War armies, became standard household fare by the 1880s. Middle-class women could purchase ready-made clothing for the whole family by the turn of the century. Bread was easier to buy than to bake. Like the new washing machines, these changes tended to alter, but not to eliminate, some of the drudgery of household work.

By the early 1900s, so many tasks had been removed from the home that some people feared the home itself would disintegrate. The kind of work that women did in the home had been transformed by the industrial revolution from production into maintenance. While working-class women followed their work into factories, middle-class women, some feared, faced what one writer called a "domestic void." "What a certain type of woman needs today more than anything else," noted an editor of the *Ladies' Home Journal* in 1911, "is some task that would tie her down. Our whole social fabric would be the better for it. Too many women are dangerously idle."[23]

Sentiments like these led some middle-class women to the domestic science movement that emerged at the end of the nineteenth century. Like the home economics movement of the Beechers' time, domestic science set out to rationalize women's tasks. To the earlier emphasis on efficiency and good training it added a moral purpose. The movement set out to preserve the home by teaching "right living." As it made the housewife's labor purposeful, so it would prevent her from seeking gratification outside the home. And, as a spin-off benefit, the middle-class housewife would set an example of domesticity to untutored immigrants. The founders of the Home Economics Association, meeting in Lake Placid, New York, in 1899, spoke with a crusading zeal about the possibilities of training women in the care of their home. They believed they would discourage radical thought, reinforce the incentive to strive for mobility, and sustain harmony in the work place by inhibiting strikes and discontent. With a righteousness characteristic of those who believe they have found the truth, members of the Home Economics Association set about educating the women of America.

The movement had three directions, all derived from the contemporary concern with scientific method. First, the housewife must inquire as to the nature of the problem she faced. Ellen Richards, a leader of the movement, argued for a change in "attitude of mind" which would lead women to ask of their tasks, "Can I do better than I am doing? Is there any other device which I might use? Is my house right as to its sanitary arrangements? Is my food the best possible? Have I chosen the right colors and the best materials for clothing? Am I making the best use of my time?"[24] The second step was exploration. The housewife had at her command the new frontiers of science. In the 1870s germ theory had been discovered. The housewife was to explore its implications for family hygiene and sanitation. With the support of the American Medical Association, women were adjured to cleanliness, both in their person and in their homes. The annual spring cleaning would no longer do. Control of germs demanded constant surveillance. Medical researchers also produced nutritional data. The housewife needed to understand food preparation and service in the context of these new discoveries. A knowledge of physiology might help. Colleges began to encourage women to study plant and animal biology as well as the science of home economics. These new subjects legitimized college education for women, who could now argue that education would turn them into better homemakers. Beset by rising standards and new demands on their administrative skills, homemakers turned to knowledge as if it were a panacea.

Solutions rested in the third direction of the movement: scientific management. Already in the early 1900s, Frederick Taylor's notions of increasing productivity by concentrating power in the hands of a managerial group that would determine the most efficient organization of work had spread through American industry. In 1912 Christine Frederick applied some of these ideas to household work. The housewife, she argued, should separate her managerial tasks from her physical labor. To do this she had to analyze her use of time and organize her day so as to reduce drudgery to a minimum. Lists of what had to be done would help her to estimate the amount of time involved. Each task should be reduced to its most efficient mode of accomplishment. The housewife was to keep careful account of her time, making sure that no task exceeded its allotted span. Bathing baby, for example, should take no more than fifteen minutes. Efficient and well-organized work would not only eliminate the need for servants in many households, it would, in the end, provide housewives with more time.

In fact, the domestic science movement and scientific management of the household had many contradictory results. At their best, they encouraged the use of new technology, lightening some household tasks. But for some housewives this meant that all the duties of the household now fell into their hands. Reducing or eliminating the need for household help exacerbated the isolation of women engaged in work in the home and sometimes increased the amount of time they actually spent at housework.

Patterns of Poverty

While well-off urban women experienced a declining need for their economic contributions to the household, poor women, urban and rural, discovered that industrialization and urbanization merely replaced one kind of productive labor with another. As if the clock had stopped, the labor of rural women continued, well into the twentieth century, to provide the family's food and clothing. The Sears Roebuck catalogue might offer an occasional new dress, but most farm women still made virtually all the family's clothing, baked bread, and processed all their own fruits and vegetables, meat and poultry.

Chores were only part of a woman's task. As one farm organization reminded its members in the mid-1880s, women's "judgement and skill in management may be essential to the success of her husband."[25] Among poor tenant farmers, especially in the post-Civil War South, wives, black and white, took their turn in the sugar, tobacco, and cotton fields. Family survival required young children to participate in family work. For tenant farm women, intense poverty and debt created a status not far removed from slavery. Forced to grow a cash crop in order to pay off the debts incurred in setting up a farm, they had little time for family gardens or domestic animals. They purchased food and supplies from the local merchant who immediately added another notch to their debt tally, perpetuating an endless cycle of semislavery. Rarely did even the best year eliminate debt, for a large crop simply increased the supply and caused the price of each bushel to drop.

Housework and household maintenance bore no resemblance to that of even the minimally secure urban housewife. Without such amenities as electricity (which did not reach the rural South until the government-sponsored programs of the 1930s) or running water, and tormented by debt, the work of the rural poor was hardly less than that of the colonial woman. In the 1930s, hundreds of thousands of poor rural families still lived in the South. Census takers counted three quarters of a million families in North Carolina alone in 1935.

We have a vivid portrait of these homes, passed down to us by Margaret Jarman Hagood, a sociologist who studied tenant farm families in the depression years of 1937 and 1938. She described kitchens in which "a wood stove or range, an oilcloth-covered table for preparing food and for eating, and a safe for storing and keeping food" were the only standard equipment. Houses with four rooms had not a single closet. Floors rarely had coverings of *rural poverty*

any kind. An occasional mother left the interviewer to "chase a pig out of the next room where he came in through an unscreened door." Under these conditions, houses needed constant "straightening." Cooking was an all-day chore since women had to contend with "wood stoves with fires to be built and kept going, correspondingly old-fashioned implements, larger size of families to be fed, bigger appetites of outdoor workers, the preparing of raw materials from scratch rather than using expensive, bought, semi-prepared foods, and dietary preferences which demand hot bread at every meal, home baked pies and cakes, and vegetables cooked for many hours."[26]

Urban poverty was of a different order. What could not be, or was no longer, produced at home had to be paid for with cash. For some women this meant going out to earn a living—following their work into the marketplace. This was a difficult choice unless there was a replacement in the household, since children required supervision, and wage earners depended on meals, laundry, and other household services. In homes without running water, heated by coal or wood stoves, maintaining the household required a great deal of time. A wage earner working ten to twelve hours a day, six days a week, would not be able to market, prepare adequate meals, or launder and mend clothes. Working men recognized this early in the process of industrialization. In order to obtain and preserve the services of women at home, they asked for a "family wage." "We must strive to obtain sufficient remuneration for our labor to keep the wives and daughters and sisters of our people home," warned the Philadelphia Trade Union in 1835.[27]

Most families assigned an available female—wife, daughter, or sister—the task of organizing the household and of stretching the limited incomes of the wage earners. The job was not easy. It included the rearing and disciplining of children as well as the emotional and physical sustenance of the menfolk. But most of all it required feeding and clothing a family, sometimes under the most discouraging conditions. Clothes had to be made, then made over again after the cloth had worn through. Shopping could be an endless haggle for stale bread and half-rotten vegetables.

The lower the skill level and income of the family's workers, the harder it was for a housewife to get by. Under the poorest conditions, housewifery became no more than an illusion. From at least the 1830s on, substantial portions of the laboring population of every large city lived in conditions of utter misery. In the 1840s, New York City already had a "cellar" population of poor people who lived in dark and airless basements, and by the 1860s, some twenty thousand people lived in wooden "shanty houses"—no more than pieces of clapboard knocked together— on Manhattan's Upper West Side. Even a brief description reveals how difficult "housekeeping" must have been in such an environment. A city inspector reported to an industrial commission in 1845: "In one room are found the family, chairs, usually dirty and broken, cooking utensils, stove, often a bed, a dog or a cat, and sometimes more or less poultry. On the outside, by the door in many cases, are pigs and goats and additional poultry. There is no sink or drainage, and the slops are thrown upon the ground."[28] Even when the worst of these conditions was eliminated at the end of the nineteenth century, housewives who lived in tenements could rarely afford the technology that eased the lives of more affluent women.

Higher incomes in some working-class families enabled women to benefit from some of the rapidly improving amenities of the nineteenth-century city. But the wives of even respectable workers benefited less than those of middling professional and managerial men. Pittsburgh, toward the end of the nineteenth century, offered working-class neighborhoods fewer sewers and paved streets, and a less dependable water supply, than it gave to middle-class neighborhoods. Workers tended to live close to the mills, so their wives battled constant grime and soot. Unpaved roads were more difficult to clean than those already paved, allowing household refuse and horse droppings to accumulate in the streets and producing higher rates of disease and death among the poor than among the better off.[29]

By the turn of the century, from one third to one half of the population of major cities such as Baltimore, Philadelphia, Chicago, and Boston consisted of poor immigrant families. Most of these lived in squalid, crowded housing. Indoor running water scarcely existed. One family might share a single toilet with three or four others. Slums were not new, but never had so large a proportion of the American population lived in such over-crowded conditions and never had housekeeping standards been so high. Housewives suffered directly from the absence of city services. To gather sufficient water for a day's washing, drinking, and cooking, they had to get up early, fill huge tubs, and haul them indoors, sometimes up several flights of stairs. The same water had to be disposed of by hauling (or pouring) it downstairs. Few working-class women benefited from washing machines, indoor toilets, or central heating. Lack of refrigeration meant daily shopping trips.[30]

Take the case of the typical Jewish immigrant woman on New York's Lower East Side in 1905. The New York State manuscript census for that year gives us a clear picture of how she lived. In three rooms—designed as bedroom, living room, and kitchen—she and her husband supported three or more children and two boarders who might be distantly related. Sleeping quarters for these seven people were scattered in every room of the small apartment. In this tiny space, the housewife laundered, cooked, and cleaned. She had no ice box. Her stove was still coal fired, needing regular cleaning and careful attention. When she shopped, she hunted for bargains and haggled to the last penny. When she cleaned, she battled with endless cockroaches. Her life emerges eloquently in some of the tales told by Anzia Yezierska, whose heroines recall above all the endless poverty, "how the rungs of the chairs were tied with ropes, the clutter of things on the bureau, the torn market bag with the spilling potatoes, bread and herring thrown on the bed. Everything so smelly, so dingy...."[31]

This description reflects the lives of many immigrant women. Sociologist Margaret Byington studied the families of steel mill workers in Homestead, Pennsylvania, in 1907 and 1908. An immigrant family there could survive on about $1.65 a day—$11.55 a week—in a community where an unskilled mill worker normally earned less than $10 a week. So a typical family—husband, wife, and three children—might have from one to four lodgers in their four-room house. Income from lodgers added about 25 percent to the family's income, with the wife typically shopping, cooking, and laundering for all the boarders and her own family.[32]

This situation was not unique to Homestead. Often families could not survive if only one family member earned money. Even in cases where one person's income could buy the family's bare necessities, the family frequently depended on the additional financial contributions of other members—especially its women—in order to save for a small plot of land, a home, or a farm in the West. Anthropologist Anthony Wallace records his conclusions about one small Pennsylvania mill town in the period just before the Civil War. Wives could and did work in the mill, but it was normally much more lucrative for them to work at home by taking in boarders. Single people needed places to live, and three or more boarders could provide as much income as an entire family could earn at the mill. A family unit, whether headed by a male or a female, could not maintain itself comfortably without the combined mill earnings of a few members and the additional income provided by boarders.[33]

This pattern of housewives' monetary contributions characterized working-class families throughout the nineteenth and into the early part of the twentieth century. In New York in the 1850s, between one quarter and one third of all Irish wives took in boarders. In Homestead, Pennsylvania, which offered fewer opportunities for women to earn money at the turn of the century, more than 40 percent of the families had at least one paying boarder. Even in Buffalo, with its numerous small industries, more than 10 percent of married Italian housewives took in boarders.[34] These contributions often went uncounted, even by the women's own families. A fourteen-year-old girl asked her newspaper's advice about whether she should drop out of school to help support the family. "My father who is a frail man," she wrote, "is the only one working to support the whole family." Explaining that she wanted to help her parents she continued, "My mother is now pregnant, but she still has to take care of the three boarders we have in the house." Like the census takers who never counted caring for boarders as work, this young woman overlooked about 25 percent of the family's income when she overlooked her mother's labor.[35] In many households a housewife's earning power was essential. Coupled with her ability to manage scarce resources, shop wisely, sew the family's clothes, and mend carefully, it made the difference between sheer survival and climbing out of poverty.

Under these circumstances, efforts of middle-class women to train immigrant wives took on a desperate poignancy. Through church groups, settlement houses, and women's clubs, but especially through schools, crusaders for domestic reform urged habits of character that were thought to sustain American values. Thrift was most important—the penny savings bank its visible symbol. Next came cleanliness, cooking from scraps of meat, and sewing. As useful as these lessons might have been in a less poverty-stricken context, they took on aspects of the absurd when they confronted the realities of many immigrant lives. Classes in domestic manners had no place where people crowded in on each other. Lessons in setting the table were irrelevant where households did not have enough knives and forks to go around. Did beds need to be made and corners squared where one boarder tumbled in as another tumbled out? Higher incomes and greater economic security would be required before immigrant women could pay attention to such things.

Yet their children listened. One woman, interviewed about her early years in America, described what she learned about manners in night school. "We wore long skirts.... And of course we were not allowed to lift it too high, only allow a little bit of the shoe to be seen. And [the teacher] used that as an example of our behavior in life. That we should be careful not to get any modernness."[36] Barbara Ehrenreich and Deirdre English, authors of *For Her Own Good*, recount the tale of an immigrant child struggling with her mother after World War II. Recalling her domestic science class, the woman commented:

I can remember the smell of ammonia—they were teaching us to clean rugs. Who had rugs? What came across was this idea that your home environment was no good and *you* had to make it different. For example, we learned that the only right way to cook was to cook everything separately.... Things all mixed together, like stews, that was considered peasant food. I would never have admitted to my teacher that my family ate its food mixed together....
The domestic science class taught us to make the beds a certain way,

with "hospital corners." That's what it's all about, right, neatness and folding? While at home you just took the sheets and shoved them under.... Then I would criticize my mother and she would really get mad at me and say, "This isn't a fancy house." Now that I think back, that's more or less what my mother and I fought about all the time. We were fighting about how life should be in the home.[37]

Post-War Prosperity

Some resolution of these problems eventually emerged out of rising levels of prosperity. The huge influx of pre-World War I immigrants settled in and began to climb up the occupational ladder. Black families left their tenant farms and moved north to New York, Chicago, and Detroit, where men and women slowly entered industrial jobs, and women took on the domestic service and household work. The job structure shifted, making more clerical and white-collar slots available. Problems of poverty remained endemic, yet, increasingly, they were perceived as individual. With limited mortgage money now available, some black and immigrant families began to buy houses; they became the example for all to follow. Perhaps most important, manufacturers discovered the home as a market for their products.

These changes induced some of what is now seen as the frenzy of the twenties. In an era of seemingly boundless optimism and of apparently endless abundance, families changed their living styles in order to participate in the surge to possess consumer goods. Robert and Helen Lynd captured the essence of the change in an anecdote they reported in their classic study of *Middletown*. A working-class mother of five, the Lynds reported, complained that her eleven- and twelve-year-old daughters were "so stuck up I can't sew for them anymore." To compensate, she had tried to get work outside the home in order "to hire their sewing done."[38] This transition from producer to consumer in the life of one woman reflects a general social trend. As the idea of consumption spread into the kitchens and closets of every home, it increased pressure on family income. To help to meet this pressure, women's economic function was further transferred from that of producer to that of consumer. Some women could meet the new demands on them by effective purchasing. Others would need to share the role of wage earner in order to maintain their family's living standards.

Massive advertising campaigns encouraged consumerism. The 1920s developed installment buying to a fine art. And with ads directed at women who were unclear now about home functions, consumer sales soared. The development of mass media helped. Movies and radio conveyed impressions of well-run homes and happy housewives, providing a model for all women. The *Ladies' Home Journal* and *Good Housekeeping* appeared in one out of every three or four homes. Like advertising, the media created images of women who did housework incidentally, devoting their "free time" to playing with children, soothing husbands, and participating in an active social life. The media also created images of dress and behavior that penetrated the ethnic life styles of many groups and induced at least an attempt at meeting newly imposed standards.

The results were, of course, uneven. Poor women suffered the indignity of not being able to provide any of the consumer goods. Working-class housewives went out to work to keep up payments on their new refrigerators and vacuum cleaners. Those who were better off raised their housekeeping standards to fill the time made available by labor-saving devices. Women turned to "experts" for advice. Children and diet were the main objects of attention. Advocates of strict discipline vied with professionals recommending permissive child rearing for control over the mother's mind. And if most women substituted canned vegetables and store-bought bread for the homemade variety, they spent more time worrying about balanced meals and attractive appearance, and even dressed for dinner.

New household technology ultimately penetrated most economic barriers. By the end of the twenties, two thirds of all households had electricity. In Middletown, where 99 percent of all homes were wired for electricity in 1925, one quarter still lacked running water, and many more did not yet have indoor bathrooms. But a home without plumbing might nevertheless contain a vacuum cleaner or an electric iron. Initially welcomed for its ability to reduce household dependence on the servant and to free mothers to pay attention to the "higher values" of the home, the new technology had its own imperative. In reducing household drudgery, it offered the possibility of liberating some women from household tasks altogether.

Most women, as Joann Vanek has pointed out, did not take advantage of it at first. They raised their standards of cleanliness, entertained more at home, cooked more elaborate meals, and probably increased the hours they spent working in their homes.[39] But the steadily increasing numbers of married women who went out to earn a living from the 1920s on testify to the fact that many housewives found servicing their homes increasingly unsatisfactory and uneconomical. Despite strong pressures urging women to stay at home, more and more women found that the cost of buying and maintaining the new technology required an extra income. Most could no longer earn this income at home, by taking in boarders or home work. They were encouraged to seek wage work by a depression-born trend to shorter workdays, which reduced the length of the workday from ten hours to eight or even less. So more and more women went to work outside the home.

Shifts in population encouraged women to continue in this direction. They could more easily satisfy family needs by engaging in wage work than by staying at home. By the 1920s more families lived in or near cities with available jobs. The size of the average family fell as the birthrate dropped by nearly a third in three decades. Child rearing could be completed in less than twenty years of a lengthening life span. Young adults moved out of their parents' houses, creating the "empty nest" syndrome. Aged parents rarely lived with children. Already by the 1930s, the pressures on married women to seek paid employment were becoming irresistible. Yet prevailing social thought still declared women to be, above all, homemakers, and into the 1950s, magazines like *Life* and *Look* applauded the "wondrous creature [who] marries younger than ever, bears more babies and looks and acts far more feminine than the 'emancipated' girl of the 1920's or even '30's." How was this contradiction to be resolved? Were women to creep into the labor force quietly, "less towards a 'big career' " as *Look* noted, "than as a way of filling a hope chest or buying a new home freezer?"[40] Historical changes in the labor force would provide new answers to that question.

THREE:
Working for Wages

IN THE LATE EIGHTEENTH CENTURY, the invention of the spinning jenny and the development of motor-driven machinery culminated in Samuel Slater's factory on the Pawtucket River in Rhode Island. The factory united the major spinning processes that prepared yarn for the weaver. Slater's factory, opened in

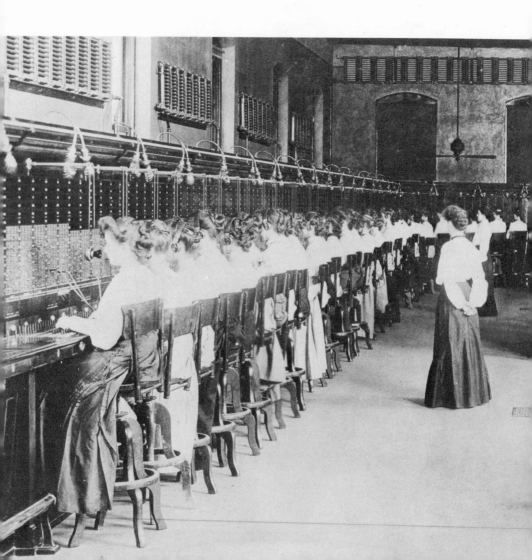

1793, was by no means the first. We have records of woolen and cotton spinning mills that employed two hundred and more women and boys in the eighteenth century.[1] Most of these relied on a combination of people who worked at home and a few employed within a factory building. Slater's mill signaled the start of a move to consolidate a variety of different manufacturing processes under one roof. If the processes were to happen inside the manufactory, as it was then called, women would have to go there too.

Factories needed workers. Yet factory work was not viewed kindly by a population committed to the pastoral values of Jefferson's sturdy yeomen. Jefferson himself had once urged that

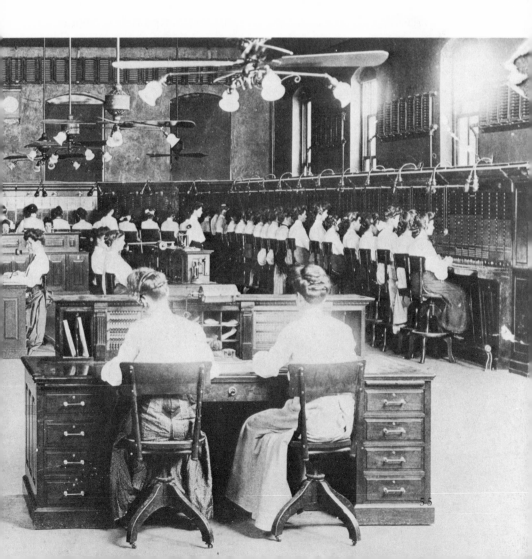

Americans "keep our workers in Europe," and he had publicly
hoped that "all our citizens would be husbandmen."[2] Visions of
Europe's dreary workshops danced in the heads of a skeptical
public when Alexander Hamilton asserted that national self-
sufficiency required the development of industry. Hamilton's
Report on Manufactures, issued in 1791, met the enthusiastic
response of only a few visionaries enamored of new ways of
harnessing power. It took a revolutionary struggle in France and
the Napoleonic wars that followed to generate widespread
support for manufacturing industries. Afraid of being permanently dependent on Europe for necessary goods and aware now
of the difficulty of obtaining imports, Jefferson acknowledged
the need for some industry. At the same time, enterprising local
artisans began to recognize the potential for profits in tapping
some of the new sources of energy.

Incipient manufacturers could, and did, import skilled crafts-
people for some jobs. They required as well a pool of dependable
workers for relatively unskilled jobs. Slater at first sought his
employees from among New England farmers dispossessed by
rising indebtedness. He hired whole families who were eager to
save money to outfit themselves for the trip west. And, as
Hamilton had proposed in his *Report on Manufactures,* Slater
sought out widows and children who "are rendered more useful
by manufacturing establishments than they otherwise would
be."[3] This method of staffing mills persisted through the early
part of the nineteenth century. But it never provided a sufficient
number of workers. Removing women from their homes did not
prove appealing to a largely agrarian population with a coherent
conception of women's roles, and independent farmers were
reluctant to adapt to the discipline of the factory. Mill owners
complained constantly that they could not find an adequate
labor supply.[4]

Creating a Labor Force

The unmarried daughters of New England farmers seemed to be
the only alternative work force. A gradual narrowing of necessary work to be performed at home had been accompanied by a

search for alternative ways in which women could contribute to the household economy as well as to their own survival. Historians sometimes talk about this process as one in which women "followed" their work out of the house and into the factory. It is certainly true that many women, finding their work at home insufficiently remunerative, went out to work or took in for pay the work distributed by the new manufactures.

It is also true that the new manufacturers desperately needed a labor force. Many of the jobs to be done were "women's" jobs in the sense that women had traditionally done them. Yet to put women into factories threatened to undermine the home. Not only did household chores require women's attention, but the nurturing and giving qualities associated with wifehood and motherhood might be eradicated by the struggle to earn a living.

This tension emerged full force only in the early nineteenth century, for as long as the vast majority of women earned their livings by going out to service, their jobs reinforced the values of home life. As the demand for nondomestic labor increased, *key* reconciling the conflict between the need for women workers and the need to keep the "home" intact became a major determinant of where and how women should work.

Could one reconcile the moral imperative of the home with the use of young women in factories? It was the genius of Francis Cabot Lowell to conceive of a way of doing so. He appealed to the young single daughters of farm families to fulfill their family responsibilities by engaging in hard work away from home. For the mill which finally opened in Lowell, Massachusetts, in 1821, he proposed carefully supervised boardinghouses for girls who would spend a few years at the loom before marriage. He offered relatively high salaries, part of which could readily be saved for a trousseau, to help pay off a mortgage, or to send a brother through college. At the same time, parents were assured that their daughters would experience hard work and discipline. A few years in the factories at high pay would make them into better wives and mothers. The mills at Lowell and elsewhere in *male based and religious* New England attracted a reliable labor force that was easily disciplined in industrial routines and was cheaper than male labor. In return, mills offered a training ground in morality.

Young women were ready for the jobs. The development of

mills coincided with, and to some extent caused, under-utilization of women in the home. At first, mills took over the spinning, and the fiber was handed out to women to weave in their homes. When weaving machinery became more complex, both processes were moved to the factory. The tremendous demand of the postrevolutionary period—when the Napoleonic wars all but cut off trade with Europe—stimulated development. Factory-made fabrics were more evenly textured and often of better quality, and it soon became cheaper for women to buy factory-made broadcloths than to weave their own.

At the same time, expanding towns up and down the East Coast encouraged farmers to produce for the market instead of for household needs. To compete in a market economy required emphasis on a cash crop as well as investment in machinery. Farmers became vulnerable to the fluctuations of the market and to competition from western lands being opened by a growing canal system. To protect themselves against these forces and to pay off their indebtedness, they were forced to rely more and more on a cash crop and to neglect the diverse operations that had made them self-sufficient. Fearful that they would lose their farms entirely, they gave up their self-sufficiency and became dependent on markets and bankers. Farmers therefore welcomed the cash relief that daughters could bring. The cumulative pattern of farm indebtedness, available female labor whose home tasks had been reduced, and a huge pent-up demand for factory goods set the stage for industrialization and, more specifically, for the movement of women into factories.

good variables to discuss

At the same time the mill owners justified their need for labor by arguing that they were providing a service for the nation. Not only could they provide the goods the nation needed, but they would "give employment to respectable women to save them from poverty and idleness." They argued that they were preserving the republican virtues of hard work and raising the moral and intellectual tone of the country.[5]

The mill girls themselves, at least in the early years, were determined to preserve their own respectability in the public eye. Aware of the degree to which they were abandoning cherished values, they insisted that they could nevertheless be "good." In one widely read fictional account, Susan Miller, who decided to go to Lowell after her father's death left the family in debt, assured her minister, "among so many there must be some who are good; and when I go there, I shall try to keep out of the way of bad company....."[6] To maintain high standards, boardinghouse residents "supervised" one another, ostracizing any with doubtful morals. Boardinghouse life built a strong sense of pride and self-respect.

But mill owners, eager to reap profits with which to repay the loans that had capitalized the industry, could not long support the high wages and good working conditions that justified wage work for independent women. By the end of the 1820s, they were already raising the amount of work women were asked to do and increasing the rates for board without increasing wages. Lowell women complained of excessively long hours, wage cuts, and extra work, as did women in mills throughout the Northeast. Finding it difficult to contribute to their families, and unable to maintain self-imposed standards of dress and education, they protested. Occasional strikes occurred, and rumblings of discontent became audible from Pawtucket, Rhode Island, to Paterson, New Jersey, and Philadelphia, Pennsylvania. In 1828, factory girls in Dover, New Hampshire, "turned out" for the first time, marching through the streets to the ridicule of onlookers. One Philadelphia paper noted that the government might "have to call out the militia to prevent a gyneocracy."[7]   *ugh!*

Conditions worsened in the 1830s. Workers complained repeatedly—to no avail. The women of Lowell struck in 1834 and again in 1836. They appealed to the revolutionary spirit of independence. "As our fathers resisted with blood the lordly avarice of the British ministry," they declared, "so we, their daughters, never will wear the yoke which has been prepared for us." And as they marched through the streets, they sang:

Oh, isn't it a pity that such a pretty girl as I
Should be sent to the factory to pine away and die?
Oh! I cannot be a slave;
I will not be a slave.
For I'm so fond of liberty
That I cannot be a slave.[8]

By 1845, Lowell workers had organized themselves into the
Female Labor Reform Association. In addition to striking, they
petitioned the state legislature for a ten-hour day. Arguing that
thirteen or fourteen hours in the mills stultified their minds,
incapacitated them for reading, and left them too fatigued for
church going, they declared that the independent character of
workers depended on shorter hours. The legislature rejected
their petition. By now the mill owners no longer argued that
hiring young women aided morality. Taking advantage of
increasing Irish immigration, they rapidly eliminated the old
work force. In 1845, only 7 percent of the employees in the eight
Lowell mills were Irish. By 1852, more than half of the work force
was foreign born. The pattern was repeated in other Massachusetts mill towns as well as in New Hampshire and in
Connecticut. The old protected New England mill "girl"
swiftly disappeared.

The pages of the *Lowell Offering*, a factory-supported paper,
reveal how completely an alternative cheap labor supply took
precedence over the employers' professed desire to serve the
country. As late as 1849, some operators continued to believe
that corporation owners would raise wages so as "to attract once
more the sort of girl who had made the industry what it was."[9]
Some felt that the mills had lost the respect of the community
because standards of morality and the old spirit of mutual
surveillance had declined. Caroline Ware, historian of the
textile industry, assesses the position of the employers. "Necessity had forced them to gain and hold the respect of the
community in order to attract the requisite workers and they
were only too eager to be relieved of that necessity by the advent
of a class of labor which had no standing in the community and
no prejudice against mill work."[10] Native-born females simply
stopped applying for jobs. In 1852, one Massachusetts paper
remarked of the Chicopee mills that "foreign girls have been
employed in such numbers that what American girls are
employed there experience considerable difficulty in finding
society among their workmates congenial to their tastes and
feelings."[11]

It is easy to exaggerate the impact of the mills. Only a tiny
fraction of women ever lived in their boardinghouses or worked

their fourteen-hour days. Only about 10 percent of all women worked in the paid labor force in the mid-1840s. Yet over half the factory population was female, and the mills depended on female labor. In textiles, shoes, and hats, women's numbers were even higher. From 80 to 90 percent of the operatives in some New England mills were women. Had the mills continued to provide the reasonable working environments that their first employees expected, they might have fulfilled their early promise, offering a continuing source of respectable employment for women. But this was not to be the case.

By the 1850s, factory work was done by immigrant women and was considered off limits for native-born Americans. But by then, so were most jobs. Even the traditional woman's occupation of domestic service had lost the solid respectability that characterized it in the colonial period. A persistent shortage of household help in colonial and postrevolutionary America had led most mistresses to treat their "help" with some respect. Equal treatment, legal protection, and tasks shared with the householder added up to expectations of "something better" for the servant. When these expectations were heightened in the early part of the nineteenth century by the postrevolutionary fervor for egalitarianism, they produced tension. The subordinate role of the servant conflicted with expectations of equality generated by revolutionary activity.

In tacit acknowledgment of the strain, the word "servant" all but disappeared from the vocabulary, except as it applied to blacks. Instead, white household workers were called "helps."[12] But more tangible evidence of dissatisfaction appears in the changing composition of the body of household workers in the period before the Civil War. As the taint of subordination led women to seek jobs in factories, schools, and stores—opportunities presented by urbanization and the rise of manufactures— the servant population as a whole rapidly metamorphosed into one of black and immigrant women.

The transition in the servant and factory populations occurred at the same time as the emergence of an urban middle class. The relatively leisured lives of the women of this group contrasted sharply with the daily existence of those who had to earn their own livings. The division between the two was justified by what historians have come to call the "domestic code." This code established proper roles for women that regulated the behavior of the well off and toward which poor and immigrant women could only aspire.

The Domestic Code

The source of this major ideological transition remains imperfectly understood, but its elements are fairly clear. Industrialization and urbanization slowly increased the number of men who worked in impersonal factories. Because men were removed from contact with children during the lengthy and exhausting day, women assumed responsibility for training children to fill future labor force needs. Simultaneously, the old puritan ethic which stressed morality, hard work, and community gave way to laissez faire economic policies that emphasized individualism, success, and competition. Men who worked hard and strove for success required wives who were emotionally supportive and who could competently supervise the household. We have already looked at the impact of this ideology on household roles. It had an equally significant effect on the work place.

In its most dramatic form, the developing ideology described the female as functioning only within her crucial sphere. Historian Aileen Kraditor notes, "It was not that social order required the subordination of women, rather...it required a family structure that involved the subordination of women."[13] One popular nineteenth-century schoolbook argued, "When a woman quits her own department...she departs from that sphere which is assigned to her in the order of society, because she neglects her duty and leaves her own department vacant...."[14] Though many strong voices objected to the constraints, they received little support from the majority of middle-class women who were persuaded that they were functioning usefully. In return for an ideology that glorified their roles and perhaps offered some power within the family, women gave up a broad range of social and economic options. By the mid-1850s, the only sanctioned occupations for "respectable" women were

important distinction [handwritten marginalia]

teaching and, when genteel poverty struck, dressmaking—done in the privacy of the home. A talented and lucky few might earn their livings at writing.

Rigid restrictions on outside activity left little room for wage earning. By defining the role at home as the measure of respectability, the domestic code sharpened class differences. It excluded from respectability most women who had to work in the paid labor force at some time in their lives, and it encouraged women to demonstrate their virtue and morality through their families. Factory work and domestic service slid further down the status scale. Immigrants, black women, and any others who toiled at necessary jobs could not hope to achieve success. Their presence in the labor force placed them outside the ranks of respectability and subjected them to all the exploitation of the industrial wage earner.

Employers derived a series of continuing benefits from the existence of the middle-class feminine code of domesticity. The code encouraged compliant behavior among women who, convinced for the most part that their real calling lay in marriage and child rearing, had only a transient interest in their jobs. The desire for respectability provided working women with a set of aspirations, equivalent to upward mobility for men, which limited their identification with workers' interests and mitigated complaints about present exploitation. A Knights of Labor organizer Leonora M. Barry summed up the problem in 1887. "If there is one cause more than another that fastens the chains on...working women it is their foolish pride, they deeming it a disgrace to have it known that they are engaged in honest toil."[15]

The belief that women belonged at home permitted employers to exploit working women by treating them as though their earnings were merely supplemental. Until the end of the nineteenth century, women customarily received about one third to one half of the prevailing male wage, a sum seldom sufficient even for a single woman to support herself. Statisticians in the late nineteenth century invented the notion of a living wage—the equivalent of our poverty-level standard of living. Economist John Commons estimated that only 25 percent of all female wage earners made a living wage in 1914—a figure placed at $8 a week. Half of all women wage earners took home less than $6 a week. And few women could count on year-round employment. Most were out of work about 20 percent of the year, reducing their wages even more.[16] Because employers assumed that a woman belonged at home, they relied on her family to make up the difference between what she earned and what she could live on. Hiring policy took this into account. Department store managers refused to engage salesclerks who did not live in families, for fear that financial need would drive them to prostitution. Employers who were convinced that women belonged at home refused to train them to perform skilled jobs, exacerbating their poverty and offering them no choice but to remain unskilled labor.

Employers also benefited from competition between men and women, which they fostered by maintaining different wage scales. Working men argued that women workers held wages down. If women were excluded from the work force, they argued in the 1830s, men's wages would be higher. In 1836, a National Trades Union Committee urged that female labor be excluded from factories. After explaining that the natural responsibility and moral sensibility of women best suited them to domesticity, the report argued that female labor produced "ruinous competition...to male labor," the final result of which would be that "the workman is discharged or reduced to a corresponding rate of wages with the female operative." The report continued:

One thing...must be apparent to every reflecting female, that all her exertions are scarce sufficient to keep her alive; that the price of her labor each year is reduced; and that she in a measure stands in the way of the male when attempting to raise his prices or equalize his labor, and that her efforts to sustain herself and family, are actually the same as tying a stone around the neck of her natural protector, Man, and destroying him with the weight she has brought to his assistance. This is the true and natural consequence of female labor when carried beyond the family.[17]

The president of the Philadelphia Trades Association advised women to withdraw altogether from the work force. "The less you do, the more there will be for the men to do and the better they will be paid for doing it, and ultimately you will be what you ought to be, free from the performance of that kind of labor which was designed for man alone to perform."[18]

Male fears of displacement or of reduced wages seemed justified. While men and women normally did not compete for the same jobs, employers often substituted one for the other in response to changing technology and labor market conditions. The process worked both ways. New England textile factories, whose workers were 90 percent female in 1828, had only 69 percent female workers in 1848. Yet more often it seemed that women replaced men. Partly as a result of the Civil War, the proportion of Massachusetts teachers who were male had dropped from about 50 percent in 1840 to 14 percent in 1865.[19] And that trend was to continue. By 1865, the labor press was complaining of "a persistent effort on the part of capitalists and employers to introduce females into its various departments of labor heretofore filled by the opposite sex."[20] The feared consequence would be to bring down the price of labor "to the female standard, which is generally less than one half the sum paid to men." Employers sometimes trained women to act as strikebreakers. According to a Senate report, a Chicago newspaper publisher "placed materials in remote rooms of the city and secretly instructed girls to set type and kept them there until they became sufficiently proficient to enter the office...."[21] Silk manufacturers testified in 1910 that "as long as there are women horizontal wrapers...[the manufacturers have] a strong defense against the demands of the men.[22]

A further effect of the domestic code was to keep women out of unions. If men faced difficulties in trying to organize, women, who believed that their real commitment was to the home, had tremendous obstacles to overcome. Since many felt their work life to be temporary, women had little incentive to join each other in a struggle for better conditions. Leonora Barry complained in 1889 that in the absence of immediate discomfort, the expectation of marriage blinded many women to the long-range advantages of unions.[23] Even women who leaned toward unionization found the hostility of employers and of male co-workers frightening. Because unions would negate the advantages of low wages and docility, employers would not tolerate them. A government report issued in 1910 noted that the moment a woman joined a union, "she diminishes or destroys what is to the employer her chief value. Hence the marked objection of employers to unions among women."[24]

Men's attitudes toward organizing women varied with their particular circumstances. Some felt keenly the competition engendered by employers who used women as strikebreakers or to undercut wages. Frequently they saw clearly that women were played off against men in the nineteenth-century labor market. Instead of repudiating conventional ideas about the social role of women, they tried to keep women out of the labor market or to confine them to limited kinds of jobs. They occasionally offered support to women attempting to unionize. In the 1830s, Baltimore journeymen tailors, New York bookbinders, and Massachusetts cordwainers all encouraged their female counterparts to unite for better working conditions. The National Labor Union, in the late 1860s, persistently urged women to organize, and the Knights of Labor, in its halcyon period in the early eighties, organized about 50,000 women into local units.[25] But just as often, men struck to protest the hiring of females. Well into the twentieth century, many craft unions had constitutions that called for suspending members who trained or worked with women.

Women who repeatedly, and often successfully, organized themselves throughout the nineteenth and early twentieth century still faced the problem of securing recognition for their unionizing efforts. As national union structures developed at the turn of the century, male trade unionists often refused to admit their sisters to national membership. Philadelphia candy workers, Norfolk waitresses, and New York printers pleaded in vain for admission to their respective national unions. If the men did not reject them outright, they procrastinated until the women succumbed to employer pressure. Toward the end of the century, some unions relented. Since women were working anyway, they argued, it was safer to have them in unions than outside them. The International Typographers admitted women under duress in 1869, and the Cigar Makers began to admit them when competition threatened their own jobs.

The domestic code, or the "cult of true womanhood," glorified the family structure and contributed to a stability that encouraged, even coerced, the male to work harder in order to support his family. For one's wife to be working meant that the husband had failed. To many men, the independence of a wife who earned money must have been threatening. The need to secure the wife's position on a pedestal helped to isolate men in an endless search for upward mobility and financial success. The idea that women should be able to stay at home, the better to mother their children, justified hard work, long hours, economic exploitation, and a host of other evils for male workers. A *New York Post* writer in 1829 accurately summed up a prevailing attitude when he asserted that the only way to make husbands sober and industrious was to keep women dependent by means of insufficient wages.

The moral imperative that confined women to their homes served many purposes. It maintained social order by providing stable families. It kept most married women and many unmarried women out of the labor force, restricting them to supportive roles in relation to the male work force. It offered industry the services of an unpaid labor force at home whose primary task was to stretch male wages. It helped to ensure that those women who did earn wages would stay in the labor force only briefly, remaining primarily committed to their families and satisfied with low-paid jobs. The special position of women as the least-paid and least-skilled members of the work force induced hostility from unskilled male labor. Afraid that women might take their jobs, some workingmen might have been afraid to demand justice from intransigent employers.

Limited conceptions of women's sphere most immediately and urgently affected women who were entirely responsible for supporting themselves and their families. Forced into the lowest-paid and most menial jobs, women who had to earn a living drifted into urban areas and factory towns. Long before the Civil War, they constituted a large class of "unemployed." In 1845, the *New York Daily Tribune* estimated that there were probably about twice as many women seeking work as seamstresses "as would find employment at fair wages." These 10,000 women, the *Tribune* concluded, constituted an oversupply of workers who could not possibly earn enough to keep themselves alive. "One and a half to two dollars per week," it declared, "is represented as the average recompense of good work-women engaged at plain sewing, and there are very many who cannot, by faith and diligence, earn more than a dollar a week."[26]

Most other occupations were no better. Artificial flower makers could earn up to three dollars and fifty cents a week at the end of the nineteenth century—less than half of what an unskilled male might make. And the trade was structured so that employers hired eleven- or twelve-year-old girls, to whom they promised to teach the skill, at seventy-five cents to one dollar a week. After they had served their time, they were fired and new "apprentices" hired—also at seventy-five cents a week. Match-box workers got five cents per gross—a margin so narrow that women who had to buy flour to paste the boxes together could do so only at a net loss. Cap makers earned about thirty cents a day, and their work conditions were so notorious that the *Tribune* wondered why they did not all "become degraded and brutalized in taste, manners, habits, and conversation." Book folders and bookbinders were said to come from a "better class." Since nine tenths of those who worked at this trade in New York boarded with their families, their poverty was not so visible. The number of "Americans" in a trade measured its relative worth. Printing and skilled millinery, relatively well-paid professions, engaged few immigrant women.[27]

The *Tribune*'s solutions to this dilemma of an oversupply of women were simple. Given their way, the editors would send women west, where there were men available. Sporadically the *Tribune* suggested subscription drives for traveling funds. Alternately, the field of female employment could be widened—for example to stores, which were not yet accustomed to using women as salesclerks.

The women themselves had other options. They could apply for relief to the local almshouse, an institution that the *Tribune* described in 1845 as "choking with the fierce assaults of shivering and famished beggary." They could turn to crime, or they could earn their livings by prostitution. What finally turned public attention to the frightening state of wage-earning women was the shocking number who chose the last. The connection between low wages and prostitution was unavoidable. One authority, Dr. William W. Sanger, wrote that in 1857, 60 percent of the inmates in New York's Blackwell's Island workhouse were female. The penitentiary was 27 percent female, and the almshouse was 55 percent female. Sanger, who was a resident physician at Blackwell's Island, went on to estimate that the majority of the female inhabitants of Blackwell's Island were prostitutes—ranging from 50 percent of those in the almshouse to close to 100 percent of those in the penitentiary.[28] Preventing women from turning to prostitution required not only appropriate ways of earning a living, but livings that paid appropriate wages. Virginia Penny completed two volumes on job possibilities for women in 1861. "When I learn," she wrote in the preface to Think and Act, "how many women have, from want and ignorance of any worthy occupation...fallen victims to the wily snares of wicked men, how many have sunk into woe and wretchedness, degradation and ruin, I would urge all girls who have it in their power...to learn some business, trade or profession."[29]

The women who "sunk into woe and wretchedness" did not necessarily believe they were falling into vice. Rather, they seemed to look upon prostitution as a necessary way of stretching income or of making up wages lost by unemployment. Somewhat later, a government investigation concluded with some surprise that because a woman had "earned money in this way does not stamp her as 'lost.' She looks upon it as an episode in her life, not as a cataclysm."[30]

Whether or not a woman actually became a prostitute was irrelevant to many respectable women who believed that engaging in paid labor was evidence enough of loose morals. Young wage-earning women often went to great pains to prove they were of good character, and by the late nineteenth century some investigators set out to help them by tabulating the numbers of wage-earning women who actually became prostitutes. To their surprise, investigators discovered that nearly a third of the 3,866 prostitutes they interviewed had been "in service"—either in private homes or in hotels and restaurants. Another third reported that they had never worked for wages. The rest came from a variety of unskilled and underpaid occupations.[31] The figures demonstrated that other people's homes were not necessarily conducive to sustaining a working woman's virtue and supported the contention that poverty bred prostitution. The study raised serious questions about a society that willingly subjected some women to live as outcasts in order to preserve the morality of the influential citizens who simultaneously used women and condemned them.

From Family Worker to Wage Worker

The domestic code set the stage for most of the nineteenth century. Most women worked for wages only reluctantly. Excluding those who worked on farms, less than 20 percent of all women could be found in the paid labor force at any one time before 1900. But the end of slavery after the Civil War and the influx of immigrant groups that followed, slowly altered the composition of the available work force. By the turn of the century, new groups of women were seeking wage work.

Who were the women who entered the labor force? Given social restrictions against wage work, they were likely to be poor. Necessity was the first determinant. For the most part they were women whose home situations did not provide them with adequate means for earning their livings. The vast majority were single women—grown-up daughters from households where an extra pair of hands was not needed as much as extra income. In the early part of the nineteenth century, these women were generally the sixteen- or seventeen-year-old daughters of New England farmers. But by its end, they were far more likely to be the children of immigrants who lived in urban households that could be managed by one person. The thirteen-year-old, who in an earlier day might have been kept on a farm to help around the dairy and to care for young children, was sent out to work. She could add to the family income and relieve the ever-present threat of unemployment and low wages.

Such family budgets as have survived for the years before World War I reveal the inability of families of unskilled male workers to exist without several wage earners. The following chart describes the source of income for ninety families of Homestead, Pennsylvania, in 1907.[32]

	A+B+C Average Weekly Income	Average Weekly Expense	A Income from Husband	B Income from Sons	C Income from Wife & Daughters (incl. lodgers)
Slav	$13.88	$13.09	$12.08	$ .52	$1.28
Black	$17.92	$12.39	$13.27	$1.30	$3.35
English speaking/ European born	$20.53	$16.97	$16.41	$3.85	$ .27
Native born/ White	$22.93	$20.47	$18.95	$2.20	$ .58

Evidence from other localities, where women's work was more plentiful, indicates that although male wages were consistently higher than those of women, the female members of working-class households were likely to contribute a larger percentage of their income to the family purse than were their brothers.[33] This holds true for black and white women, for native-born women and those who were immigrants, and for a wide variety of ethnic groups. Under normal circumstances, these women lived at home until they married. If they left the family to earn their livings elsewhere—as black women were often forced to do—they sent large portions of their incomes back home. Their brothers, on the contrary, often received a respite of several years when they were encouraged to see if they could make their way in the world.

Since the level at which they were paid assumed women were dependent on either father or husband, the 20 percent or so of wage-earning women who had no "homes" and had to support themselves entirely were in a sad way. These were women without parents or supportive siblings. Some of them had immigrated alone. Others had never married or had outlived families. Many boarded with cousins or distant relatives. Others found refuge in lodging houses. Not until the 1920s did it become economically plausible for many women to consider moving out of their homes and into shared apartments.

Again, a look at some summary budgets is revealing. The charts on pages 74 and 75 are taken from a study of the incomes and expenses of 450 "self-dependent" working women in Boston. The figures, gathered between 1907 and 1909, reveal how difficult it was for women to live on their incomes. Except for those in the "professional" category, all run a deficit. To make ends meet, women scrimped and saved on one part or another of their expenses. Salesclerks, for example, tended to spend more heavily than other women on clothing and rent—to keep up appearances of gentility. But they saved little and probably cut down on food. In the higher income groups—professionals and office workers—the percentages spent on food and rent are reasonable. But in the lowest income groups, where the vast majority of wage-earning women were concentrated, food and rent together consumed from 50 to 80 percent of income.

The data indicate that a single woman—a woman "adrift," as she was sometimes appropriately called—could scarcely survive on a daily basis, much less put anything by for a rainy day. A group of Boston sewing women who in 1869 urged the state legislature to give them homes were of this kind. "Give us good and kind husbands and suitable homes," they argued, and they would withdraw their request. "It is no better for women to be alone, than it is for men."[34]

The widow with small children was even worse off. From the beginning, the mill towns drew a disproportionate share of such women. They worked in the mills themselves or, if they were lucky, they sent their older children to work, while they kept boardinghouses or took in laundry. Combining the income of several small earners could enable a family to get by. A study of the small mill town, Rockdale, Pennsylvania, in the 1850s, reveals that mothers as well as children entered the mill. The only consistent pattern was that one female remained at home to take care of the household. Which household members chose wage work seems to have been more a function of how the household as a whole could best produce the necessary income than of anything else. In other town, like Cohoes, New York, marriage removed women from the mills and they sought income in other ways.[35]

Married women with husbands present were still relatively rare wage earners in the 1850s, yet by 1900 they had increased to statistically significant proportions.[36] Among black women now freed from slavery and struggling to maintain their economic equilibrium in the face of vast discrimination, the luxury of sparing one family member to take care of household needs could not always be afforded. Among the poor, who were often black or immigrant, unmarried women commonly entered the work force in their teens, staying there until marriage. Some figures reveal how the lives of women began to change at the turn of the century. Of all the women over sixteen in 1880, census takers counted less than 13 percent who were working for wages in nonagricultural jobs. In 1900, they counted 17.3 percent. And by 1910, more than 20 percent of all the over-sixteen-year-old women worked for wages outside of agriculture. More than one of every five gainfully employed workers was now a women.[37]

Decisions as to which family members would work often depended on the local labor market. Even the limited number of jobs open to women were not available to all women. Family circumstance and the cultural norms of particular immigrant groups limited the kinds of jobs women would take. For example, if they could, mothers of small children avoided jobs as sleep-in servants, as they then might have to give over care of their offspring to others. Some mothers chose night work in factories so that they could care for their young in the daytime. The idea of being a servant was offensive to some women. Yankee women avoided it at all costs, as did members of many immigrant groups. "It isn't the work; it's the degradation, and I won't submit to it," said Louisa May Alcott's heroine Christie, who submitted to it after all.[38] Alcott wrote from her own experience. Confronted with her family's need for income and the absence of other employment, she took a job as a servant in 1850. Despite their financial need, the family objected strenuously. In an article called "How I Went Out to Service," Alcott wrote, "Leaving the paternal roof to wash other people's teacups, nurse other people's ails, and obey other people's orders for hire—this was degrada-

(text continued on page 76)

Average Annual Expenditures
of Women Workers by Occupation[39]

	Professional	Clerical	Sales	Factory	Waitresses	Kitchen Workers
Avg. Net Income	$695.41	$499.59	$357.34	$382.37	$364.42	$342.30
Food:						
Amount	$192.18	$174.40	$164.56	$147.75	$171.92	$156.65
% of Income	27.63	34.91	46.05	38.64	47.17	45.76
Rent:						
Amount	$80.33	$82.73	$79.70	$55.76	$53.29	$82.17
% of income	11.55	16.56	22.30	14.58	14.62	24.00
Clothing:						
Amount	$112.27	$70.43	$68.41	$70.71	$57.82	$28.22
% of Income	16.14	14.10	19.14	18.49	15.87	8.24
Health:						
Amount	$26.38	$12.44	$19.05	$23.96	$11.45	$8.64
% of Income	3.79	2.49	5.33	6.27	3.14	2.52
Savings:						
Amount	$130.41	$88.65	$38.55	$51.20	$54.55	$61.67
% of Income	18.75	17.74	10.79	13.39	14.97	18.02
Misc.:						
Amount	$142.13	$132.96	$105.93	$93.57	$61.65	$40.28
% of Income	20.44	26.61	29.64	24.47	16.92	11.77
Total Avg. Expenditure	$683.70	$561.61	$476.20	$442.95	$410.68	$377.63
Surplus of Income over Expenditure	$11.71	0	0	0	0	0
Deficit of Expenditure over Income	0	$62.02	$118.86	$60.58	$46.26	$35.23

Average Annual Expenditures
of Women by Wage Groups[40]

	$3-5 per week	$6-8 per week	$9-11 per week	$12-14 per week	$15 and over per week
Avg. Net Income	$231.36	$350.15	$493.54	$629.28	$885.31
Food:					
Amount	$134.89	$162.23	$169.70	$190.97	$205.66
% of Income	58.30	46.33	34.38	30.35	23.23
Rent:					
Amount	$49.87	$71.83	$74.81	93.66	$115.59
% of Income	21.56	20.51	15.16	14.88	13.04
Clothing:					
Amount	$50.41	$66.44	$88.99	$105.87	$108.40
% of Income	21.80	18.97	18.03	16.82	12.24
Health:					
Amount	$13.43	$18.81	$22.09	$22.91	$16.75
% of Income	5.80	5.37	4.48	3.64	1.89
Savings:					
Amount	$8.96	$7.64	$31.63	84.72	$135.91
% of Income	3.87	2.18	6.41	13.46	15.35
Misc.					
Amount	$53.43	$69.36	$117.06	$97.93	$139.21
% of Income	23.09	19.81	23.70	15.56	15.72
Total Avg. Expenditure	$310.99	$396.31	$504.28	$596.06	$721.52
Surplus of Income over Expenditure	0	0	0	$33.22	$163.79
Deficit of Expenditure over Income	$79.63	$46.16	$10.74	0	0

tion, and headstrong Louisa would disgrace her name forever if she did it."[41] Most Yankee women preferred sewing at home where the indignity of working for a living could be shrouded in privacy, even at the price of earning a tiny fraction of what they could earn at service.

Discrimination played its part in reducing job choices. For black women, domestic service often seemed a lesser evil than field work, which was frequently the only other option. Until World War I, few other jobs existed, although some employers would hire black women for menial tasks. Tobacco processors, for example, employed black women to strip tobacco—a job white women would take only as a last resort. Employers used language and race to build barriers around employees. Some garment industry factories, for example, deliberately hired women who spoke different languages to inhibit communication.

Within job categories, women considered certain jobs more acceptable than others. In department stores, among the most genteel places to work, cash girls who brought change could be children of immigrants, while salesclerks were likely to be more "refined." Waitresses, considered by many in the early twentieth century to be among the most degraded of workers, had their own hierarchies. Some chose not to work where liquor was sold, even though tips were larger.

A combination of family need, preference, and available opportunities influenced work decisions. In large cities, as Barbara Klaczynska's study of Philadelphia notes, women's work preferences were modified by the cost and distance of travel as well as by the need for family approval. Jewish women, who lived close to the garment center, almost universally worked at sewing machines. American-born white women, who had their pick of women's jobs, chose to work in department stores, among the lowest paid, yet, by repute, the most dignified, of jobs.[42]

In smaller cities such as Manchester, New Hampshire, and in the mill villages of South Carolina, kinship networks tended to determine where and when a woman worked. In these towns married women were much more likely to do wage work throughout their lives, leaving the work force for a few years when they had children, and only permanently after their children were old enough to support them. Again, the pattern differed for black women, who generally worked continuously and did not take time out from paid work during their child-bearing years. They, too, often retired when they were grand-mothers, though in contrast to the mill women, they would then take their turn at caring for children.

Buffalo's Italian women normally did not take in boarders or work in factories. But they contributed to the family income by packing up the children in the summer harvest season and picking fruits and vegetables. They managed thus to continue their family roles, without threatening their husbands or vio-lating community norms. Jews, who had few inhibitions about the kinds of jobs their daughters could take, generally kept wives out of wage-earning situations. Children were sent to work before mothers, and women's real economic contributions were disguised in "mom and pop" stores and peddlers' carts. And it was no accident that large numbers of Jewish women ended up at work behind sewing machines. Like other immigrants, they chose jobs with their compatriots. Whenever possible, those who were employed found jobs for the newly arrived who shared their language and culture.

Balanced against the restrictions they imposed on themselves was the desire of immigrant women to contribute to the economic security of their families. Primarily southern and eastern European Catholic and Jewish, new immigrants were channeled into the bursting ghettos of expanding cities. Women *An ethic* from peasant societies, whose traditions incorporated both strong family loyalty and strong work orientations, saw little need to play confined roles. Wherever they could, they struc-tured their lives so that paid work became plausible.

Unenviable Jobs

If poverty, especially urban poverty, meant that a woman could contribute more by her earning power than by her attempts to

(text continued on page 80)

Women in the Paid Work Force

Prior to the nineteenth century, most women who needed to earn money went "out to service," doing domestic work in other people's homes. With the development of manufacturing, women began to work in factories, and then, late in the nineteenth century and in the twentieth century, in offices, stores, and hospitals as well. Women, like men, entered the work force because they needed to earn money to help support themselves and their families. Almost always, they worked separately from men and for much lower wages. Top left: weighing wire coils. Top right: secretarial work, c. 1900. Bottom: sewing, in a sweatshop.

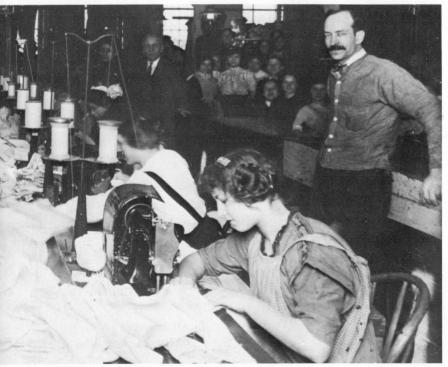

stretch the scarce resources of a household, then a job was a practical necessity. Women who need to work for economic reasons have constituted and still constitute the vast majority of wage-earning women in America. By 1900 almost 50 percent of all wage-earning women outside agriculture were either immigrants or their daughters. Another 15 percent were black women. Native-born white women, who made up about 55 percent of the female population, were only about 35 percent of the gainfully employed women.

In a restricted job market, women forced to work balanced their own preferences and desires against the options available to them. Most settled for unenviable jobs. In 1900, about 33 percent of women workers were domestic servants or waitresses. Nearly 25 percent worked in factories and mills. Ten percent worked in agriculture. Less than 10 percent were saleswomen or clerks, and a more fortunate 10 percent were professionals. The remaining 12 percent or so of wage-earning women worked in their own homes as laundresses, dressmakers, seamstresses, and boardinghouse keepers. A sprinkling were telephone operators.

Those who worked as servants were perhaps the least envied of all female wage earners. A late nineteenth-century maid of all work might be expected to clean the entire house and iron and mend. She might also launder all the clothes and prepare, serve, and clean up after three meals a day. To this would often be added such tasks as baking bread, watching children, shopping, and attending to sick members of the household. All this when many households still had coal-fired stoves that required daily attention and biweekly cleaning and that increased the soot and grime; when irons were heavy instruments that calloused the hands; when vacuum cleaners were nonexistent; and when food preparation still included preserving fruits, making jams, and putting up pickles.[43]

The lot of the servant probably reached its nadir around the turn of the century—just before household appliances came into widespread use and yet sufficiently after their introduction to persuade many women that they could get by with little help. Advancing household technology, which might have relieved the servant's lot, probably made it worse. Sometimes chores that had been removed from the household in an earlier period, such as washing and ironing, were returned to it as gas and electrically powered machinery became available. Mistresses used technology to reduce the number of servants while increasing the number of tasks to be done. And sometimes they demanded personal service as well. Since the overwhelming majority of domestic servants in this period worked in families where they were the only servant, the entire burden of household work fell on their shoulders. Small wonder then that as factory work became more widely available, women often chose not to be servants.

Mistresses professed themselves mystified by the dearth of help that resulted. "What is the cause of this boycott of household employment on the part of wage-earning young women?" asked the YWCA'S Commission on Household Employment in 1915.[44] Citing the advantages of "healthful" work, free from the pollutants of a factory environment and imbued with the morality of home life, potential mistresses tried to attract women into domestic work. They wanted to solve their servant problems and save the young from the malign influences of shop and factory at the same time. They failed. Not even relatively high wages attracted women into domestic work. Before 1900, a good general houseworker might earn around $3 a week with room, board, uniforms, and all expenses taken care of. Although this was probably higher than a beginning factory worker could earn after she had paid for board, transportation, clothing, and the like, it did not induce women into domestic work. For one thing, servants could not normally expect to "advance" in their field. Nor did salaries rise significantly with experience.

Other attempts to attract women into domestic service were equally unsuccessful. By 1899 the Committee on Domestic Reform of Boston's Women's Educational and Industrial Union, having carefully surveyed hundreds of factory workers, concluded that three obstacles prevented them from entering domestic work: money, social stigma, and long hours. All these, the committee concluded, could be resolved by training young women who would then, as skilled workers, command higher wages, be able to regulate their hours, and presumably receive the respect due their skill. In 1899 they founded a school for domestic servants. For $72 tuition and board, it offered an eight-month course that included a three-month apprenticeship for which the servant got $2 per week. Courses covered such subjects as kitchen work, including care of the fire, care of sinks, making plain soups, tea, coffee, chocolate, and cocoa; laundry work, including plain washing and ironing and general care of bed and table linen; chamber work, which included sweeping and dusting; and parlor work, with attention to answering the doorbell properly. The final grade determined wages on graduation. An "A" rated the student $4 per week. A "B" student would earn $3.75; a "C" student, $3.50; and a "D" student would only receive $3.25 a week.[45]

The women who would not be servants were unimpressed. They saw the problem in the structure of the job, not in their own intransigence or poor training. Servants, they argued, gave up any possibility of independence. They were always at the beck and call of a mistress. Their hours were endless and subject to whim. They were lonely. They had little time or opportunity to socialize, and few homes offered them a place to receive their friends. They had no chance to "improve" themselves, as time to go to school was rarely granted. One factory worker summed up her refusal to consider domestic service in a succinct sentence. "A domestic seems to be a sort of slave to her employer, while the factory girl's time is her own after a certain hour."[46]

Resistance of women to the lack of independence and their insistence on regular hours contributed to a change in the structure of the occupation. What had before 1900 been a "sleep-in" occupation slowly transformed itself to one where women were more and more often hired by the day. The introduction of labor-saving devices helped too—enabling housewives to do with less "help" than might have been possible earlier. Huge numbers of women left housework altogether, as opportunities to move into other jobs presented themselves. They took jobs as laundry workers in commercial laundries, as aides in hospitals, as food preparers and servers in commercial kitchens. They benefited from regular hours, defined duties, and social companionship on the job. But they continued to work in jobs that made life easier for housewives. They were doing outside the home for large numbers of households what they had done inside the home for one household at a time.

Those who continued to work inside homes found that removing certain tasks left them with only rote work such as scrubbing, dusting, and scouring. As the job deteriorated further, it attracted women who were excluded, by discrimination, from other sectors of the labor market. In 1900, black women, who constituted less than 20 percent of the female population, were 23 percent of the servants in large cities. By 1920, they were nearly 40 percent of the urban servant population. As the numbers of immigrant women decreased and their daughters found alternate jobs, the proportion of black women in a declining servant population rose.[47]

There seems to be little question that mistresses consistently discriminated against black domestics, offering lower wages, demanding greater quantities of hard labor, and substituting food and old clothing for pay. But black women servants had never been treated with even the minimal dignity accorded to white servants. In the South, where they constituted nearly all of the servant population, and where few alternatives to starvation existed, these women were often paid next to nothing, removed from their families for weeks at a time, and given entire responsibility for running whole households. Sheer necessity forced women to accept these jobs. The depth of their need is indicated by the fact that as late as 1920, nearly one third of black domestics were married compared with less than one tenth of the total group of domestics.

In the North, women hired themselves out by the day or the hour for whatever they could get. One worker described what it was like to be on the "slave" market. "Every morning, rain or shine, groups of women with brown paper bags or cheap suitcases stand on street corners in the Bronx and Brooklyn waiting for a chance to get some work. Sometimes there are fifteen, sometimes 30, some are old, many are young and most of them are Negro women waiting for employers to come to the street corner auction blocks to bargain for their labor."[48]

The change in status of the servant from sleep-in domestic to day worker reflected the change in household structure. Compared to the sleep-in maid, the day worker gained immeasurably in personal freedom, yet she still lacked the advantages of impersonal work. Day workers got no paid holidays or sick leave. They worked an unpredictable schedule. Excluded from social security benefits until 1952 and from Federal minimum wage provisions until 1974, domestic workers labored at the lowest possible pay. Unattractive job conditions have insured that, in recent years, young household workers would continue to be recruited from among the newest and least-skilled immigrant groups. They are seen by many housewives as raw recruits to the work place, in need of discipline and ever eager to cheat the "unsuspecting" householder.

It is an open question whether women who worked in industry were much better off than servants for most of the nineteenth and early twentieth century. In cities like Philadelphia, Boston, Chicago, and New York, the large majority of those in industry earned their living sewing. They followed in an honorable but poor tradition. Sewing had emerged as a way to make a living in the cities of the 1820s, at the same time as textile mills had absorbed the daughters of New England farmers. By 1824, Matthew Carey, a Philadelphia merchant-entrepreneur, was already denouncing it. "It may excite wonder," he wrote, "how the seamstresses, spoolers, etc., are able to support human nature, as their rent absorbs over two-fifths of their miserable earnings. The fact is they generally contrive to raise their rent by begging from benevolent citizens...and, of course, their paltry earnings go to furnish food and clothing."[49] Carey estimated that some 18,000 to 20,000 women earned their livings sewing in the cities of New York, Boston, Philadelphia, and Baltimore. A woman who worked "with great expertness from sunrise till 10 or 11 o'clock at night...without any interruption whatever for sickness, or attention to their families, [could] earn a dollar and a half per week." But most women had to spend time fetching and returning the garments they were to stitch together in their homes. There was almost never enough work to go around, and the trade slacked off in the summer months. At twelve and a half cents a shirt, three or four shirts a week, the average seamstress could do little more, as poet Thomas Hood wrote metaphorically, than stitch herself a shroud.

The ready-made clothing business was dominated by women. In custom or "bespoke" tailoring, skilled male tailors made whole garments with the aid of their wives and children. Ready-made clothes, on the other hand, were cut out and distributed by wholesalers. Women took the pieces home or worked on them in the shop of the cutter. Then the garments were returned to the merchant for finishing and pressing. Since almost every woman could ply a needle, it had seemed natural for women to continue to do the work they had always done at home. Manufacturers willing to distribute goods to the home had an infinite choice of women to use—and the system lent itself to abuse. Some women complained in 1830 that low wages were partly due to "under-bidding." "Those who have a home and all the necessaries of life," quoted the *Massachusetts Journal and Tribune*, "will underbid them for the sake of buying a new belt or a new feather."[50]

Until the 1840s, clothing made in this way was almost always for men, with shirts and pantaloons being the most popular items. Then children's clothing was added, and finally in the 1850s, a few women's garments: corsets, mantillas, and cloaks. But most women's clothing could not be purchased "ready-made" until toward the end of the nineteenth century. And poor people made all of their own clothing until well into the twentieth century.

By the end of the nineteenth century, the sewing machine had come into general use. Invented in 1850, it offered to make life easier for thousands of overworked women. Instead, it tended to centralize the garment industry and to increase competition for work. Initially, merchants insisted that tailors and tailoresses rent or purchase machines in order to improve the quality of their garments. Seamstresses thus became "operators," and the garment industry began to attract large numbers of men— mostly immigrants—who competed with women for jobs. Merchants lowered piece rates to compensate for increasing productivity, and they simplified the work process further. They farmed out bundles of cloth to contractors who hired operators to make up the clothing. The contractor then returned the garments to the merchant. The contractor who cut his expenses to a minimum could underbid his competitors for the bundles and thereby get more work. He set up shop in a room of his tenement apartment, required his operators to furnish their own machines and thread, and was chary with light, heat, and space. When little work was available, the contractor cut his rates per piece to the point where operators could make a living only by working endless hours or by taking work home with them. Conditions in these shops are legendary. Women routinely worked ten hours a day, six days a week. Supervisors locked doors to prevent workers from going to the bathroom without permission. A variety of tricks cheated women of some of their meager wages. Employers turned back clocks to add extra minutes to the day or distributed tiny ticket stubs, easily lost, as tokens of work completed. Whispers of easy tasks in return for sexual favors filtered through the industry.

homework

These small shops proliferated after the Civil War. By 1900, they paralleled but had not replaced "home work" in importance. Home work remained an important source of income well into the depression of the 1930s. This kind of parallel structure characterized a number of light industries in which women represented a large proportion of the workers. In the button, cigar, and artificial flower industries, large numbers of women labored under the same sort of piecework arrangements as in the garment industry. Owners benefited from the dampening effect that home work had on the wages of all workers in the industry. Ultimately, the pressure to make work more efficient placed such processes as clothing manufacture and laundry work almost entirely within factory walls.

In other areas, where factory work characterized the industry from the beginning, conditions were often somewhat better, but wages were no higher. Mary Van Kleeck's study of New York bookbinders in 1910, for example, offered some devastating conclusions about this relatively well-regulated industry. For $7.22 a week—a wage $2 below the accepted minimum on which a woman could support herself in New York City—women operated "complicated machines, repeating one process hour after hour, standing at work all day, carrying loads of heavy paper from one part of the shop to another, stooping frequently to lift the folded sections of books, pressing a foot pedal rapidly and incessantly, bundling the completed volumes to wrap them for shipping."[51] Like other researchers, Van Kleeck concluded that fatigue, inadequate nutrition, and the additional burden of household work took its toll on these women. Their conditions were typical. Carroll Wright, then chief of the Massachusetts Bureau of Labor Statistics, found that long hours spent standing, inadequate toilet facilities, lack of ventilation, and dust particles that clogged the lungs were the normal accouterments of the wage-earning woman's life.[52]

What Is to Be Done?

It took many years, and the efforts of many reformers and trade unionists, to call public attention to these evils. Frequently reformers became concerned when they feared that young women who worked for several years under degraded, unsanitary conditions could never be fit mothers. They pointed to deformed and undernourished bodies—to characters coarsened by too much worldly contact. As employers took advantage of the plentiful immigrant labor supply to reduce wages, and coerced even harder work out of vulnerable employees, resistance emerged. Militant trade unions, bloody strikes, marches, and demonstrations drew public attention to the grievances of all workers. Newspaper exposés and government investigations noted the injurious effects on all workers, but especially on women, of harsh working conditions and of wages insufficient to keep body and soul together. Investigators worried about the morality of working women. Some pointed to spreading prostitution as one consequence of low industrial wages.

The most radical solutions came from leading feminists like Charlotte Perkins Gilman. Women's inability to earn a living, Gilman argued, was a result of her attachment to the home. Woman had never evolved in her relationship to production as man had, but had remained static from the time he began to clothe and feed her. She put it succinctly in *The Home*. "The homebound woman is clogging the whole world," she wrote there. For the sake of the progress of mankind, she argued, the home should be reorganized to make more efficient use of labor and to free women to function in economic independence.[53]

Gilman, who became a kind of hero of the first wave of feminism in the early twentieth century, contributed to the reawakening of a generation of young college women. Even before Gilman wrote, however, other middle-class women stretched out a helping hand. During the civil war, seamstresses and middle-class reformers joined together to form the Women's Protection Union (WPU). For more than thirty years, the WPU provided legal aid to wage-earning women and enabled many to collect improperly withheld wages. Susan B. Anthony helped to organize a Working Women's Association in 1869. But the skilled wage earners it attracted dropped out in less than a year. Anthony alienated many wage-earning women when some of the female printers, whose training she had supported, acted as strikebreakers against the International Typographical Union. Grace Dodge's Working Girls Clubs, founded in 1884, offer a better example. There, working-class women, carefully screened for gentility and high moral tone, met together with speakers and teachers in lectures, classes, and social events designed for "uplift." Such groups proliferated at the turn of the century. The industrial division of the YWHA provided housing, wholesome recreation, and an analysis of industrial problems. Boston's Women's Educational and Industrial Union offered vocational training of a limited sort, especially to women who wished to train as domestics. The National Consumers League and its state affiliates took sweatshop workers and department store clerks under its wing by organizing "label" campaigns. They identified products made under wholesome conditions and set up "white lists" of department stores where employees were well treated. The National Women's Trade Union League worked with the American Federation of Labor to provide the money and organizational skill that ultimately brought thousands of women into the trade union movement.

Middle-class women who organized these groups had mixed motives. In contrast to wage earners who wanted improved conditions, shorter hours, and better pay to make their lives easier, many of the more affluent women wanted to ensure the compatability of necessary paid work with the health and morality required to sustain the family. For them, preserving women's home roles remained paramount.

Other relatively affluent women became involved in protecting their wage-earning sisters for different reasons. Sometimes as a result of changes in their own lives, they came to understand the plight of working-class women. For some wealthy married women, affluence, servants, and a decline in the birth rate could easily add up to boredom. Even women from modestly comfortable families might find household duties insufficient to satisfy work needs. These women sought other sources of satisfaction. In the nineteenth century, some rejected marriage to knock on the guarded doors of medical and law schools. They entered graduate departments of economics and sociology. After the turn of the century, numbers of married women with children joined their ranks. Like Crystal Eastman and Henrietta Rodman, who became known as "New Women," they were determined to earn their bread and to live as freely as the men who earned theirs. They set themselves up as visible symbols of a new economic independence. Their perspective, and sometimes their jobs, contributed to a growing understanding of the economic necessity that drove working-class women into the work force. Eastman's first job, for example, was to investigate industrial accidents in Pittsburgh in 1909. From there she was appointed to New York State's Employer's Liability Commission where she drafted the state's first worker's compensation law.[54]

Wage-earning women chose their allies from feminists and male workers as different situations dictated. Some women became convinced that only political pressure brought by women who could vote would alleviate women's lot. They chose to join the final sweep for women's suffrage and to help forge alliances among unskilled industrial workers, male and female, to get the vote for women. For many wage earners, this was a difficult decision. Mainstream suffragists in the National American Women's Suffrage Association (NAWSA) and its predecessors had long pleaded for women's right to vote on the grounds that educated, middle-class female voters would help to counteract the votes of untutored male immigrants. Not until the turn of the century did the NAWSA take the official position that all women needed the vote to help protect themselves against the economic exploitation that threatened to undermine the home. This argument appealed to women trade unionists as well as to unskilled male workers whose daughters and sweethearts were most often found in the labor force. By viewing women's suffrage as a social extension of domestic housekeeping, suffragists built upon the thread that united women across class lines. Women should possess the right to vote because only women were moral and pure enough to protect child-rearing and homemaking functions. The assumptions about women's role on which the argument rested could later be used to justify women's shouldering of the double burden of home care and wage work. But for the moment, the vote promised wage-earning women enough political clout to force legislators to regulate working conditions.

Wage-earning women did not stop with political alliances. Despite the odds against success, they joined together in collective organizations. Most women's unions, like the Lowell Female Labor Reform Association, founded in 1845, were short lived. It was too easy to replace unskilled women with new workers. The most successful women's union after the Civil War had close contact with men's organizations. Troy's Female Collar and Laundry Workers Union, founded in 1864, built a strong alliance with the male iron molders in their town. The Women's Typographical Union, organized in New York City in 1868, accepted some skilled males from Typographical Union 6, and became a local of that union a year later. The cigar makers, afraid of female competition, reluctantly accepted women into their union in the 1870s. And in the 1880s, women joined the Knights of Labor—a powerful national federation of unions—in enormous numbers. Perhaps as many as one of every ten Knights was a woman, yet most attempts to organize proved unsuccessful. When the Knights faded away in the late 1880s, most women were left without unions. The American Federation of Labor, which succeeded the Knights as America's major federation of unions, was made up largely of skilled craftsmen reluctant to organize the unskilled at all, much less to organize unskilled women.

Given a chance to organize, women were devoted and successful union members, convinced that unionism would serve them as it served their brothers. One seventeen-year-old textile worker captured the sentiments of many. "We all work hard for a mean living. Our boys belong to the miners' union. Women must act like men...."[55] In mixed unions of men and women, women often led men in militant actions. Iowa cigar makers reported in 1899 that some striking men had resumed work, while the women were standing pat. Female boot and shoe workers in Massachusetts in 1905 were reported to be tough bargainers. "It is harder to induce women to compromise," said their president, "they are more likely to hold out to the bitter end...to obtain exactly what they want."[56] Curiously, the same family attachments that inhibited women from joining unions, encouraged a fighting spirit. Given room and board from a sympathetic family, a young, single woman could hold out longer than a man or woman with large numbers of dependents. The existence of family and community support may have been a key factor in the 1909 strike of New York City garment workers. When 20,000 mostly young Jewish women walked out of New York City's garment shops over the initial objections of the male union leadership, predictions that they could not hold out abounded. With the help of the publicity generated by the Women's Trade Union League, they maintained ranks for three long months. By then most manufacturers had signed union contracts and the "girls" breathed life into the floundering International Ladies Garment Workers Union.

Despite these impressive efforts, the campaign to organize women was tinged with failure. Only about 3.3 percent of the women engaged in industrial jobs in 1900 were organized into trade unions. The garment workers strikes in 1909–1910 doubled that figure. But still by 1920, less than one in fifteen wage-earning women belonged to a labor union. More than 20 percent of the labor force was female, yet women accounted for only 8 percent of organized workers.[57]

While a few male trade unionists made sporadic attempts to organize women into trade unions, the labor movement as a whole quickly abandoned organization in favor of legislation that would raise women's wages, lower their hours, and prescribe the kinds of jobs in which they could be employed. At its most comprehensive, the movement for what became known as protective labor legislation included regulations of sanitary conditions, such as the number of toilets per worker. It focused on workers' health, agitating for legislation to regulate ventilation, dust, and excessive heat or weight. And it frequently restricted women from working at night and in certain "immoral" environments such as bars. The campaign, which came to a head just before the First World War, brought together reformers, trade unionists, and wage-earning women in a broad coalition. To many, it seemed like a reasonable compromise between excluding women from the work force altogether, and sacrificing family roles.

The practical effects of protective labor legislation for women were mixed. Nobody could quarrel with health and safety laws that protected both men and women. But much of the legislation was directed at women alone. Working women found themselves subject to an increasing barrage of legislation limiting the hours of work, establishing minimum wages, and regulating the sanitary conditions under which they could work. These laws had the immense advantage of ameliorating the worst conditions of women's work, while offering to conserve the health and energy to rear present and future families. Their supporters quite specifically argued that legislation was in the best interests of the state. Oregon, for example, preceded its minimum wage law with a preamble: "The welfare of the State of Oregon requires that women and minors should be protected from conditions of labor which have a pernicious effect on their health and morals, and inadequate wages...have such a pernicious effect."[58] Men did not benefit from minimum wage laws in this period, and courts repeatedly struck down legislative restrictions on hours which applied to men.

At the same time, legislation had a significant impact on the work force as a whole. In reducing the economic desirability of female employees, it limited competition with males. In the words of one authority, "The wage bargaining power of men is weakened by the competition of women and children, hence a law restricting the hours of women and children may also be looked upon as a law to protect men in their bargaining power."[59] Workingmen favored minimum wage legislation for women because it effectively reduced a downward pull on their wages. In the 1920s, the newly established Women's Bureau of the Department of Labor took great pains to prove that women were not displaced by factory laws. But the evidence is contradictory. A Massachusetts employer group told the Women's Bureau that whenever women contributed less than 25 percent of a factory's labor force, the women would be let go, for "it will not pay to change the hours for the whole plant nor to keep the women and have two sets of hours...."[60] Fortunately for women, new job opportunities in white-collar areas emerged just at the moment when protective legislation became widespread. These job shifts perhaps explain why the rate at which women participated in the labor force remained stable until the late 1930s.[61]

With rare exceptions, employers did not suffer from the new laws. Legislation was slowly and tentatively achieved, with due regard for the interests of manufacturers whose businesses were likely to be hurt. Sanitary and health regulations often went unenforced. By and large, regulation was opposed only by small manufacturers represented in the National Association of Manufacturers. Their interests often contradicted those of the corporations and labor unions that both came to approve of and lobby for protecting women.

Working women were confused about the legislation, and the trade unionists among them took contradictory positions in the early years of the twentieth century, finally opting for protection when organization seemed impossible. By the 1920s, when most industrial states had some legislation limiting hours and regulating night work, conflict came to a head. Some feminists, largely business and professional women, protested the assumption that women had special roles that required state protection. They advocated an Equal Rights Amendment to the federal Constitution whose effect would be to eliminate the body of legislation so painstakingly built up. Groups representing wage-earning women, such as the Women's Trade Union League and the Women's Bureau, led the fight against the Equal Rights

Amendment (ERA).[62] One woman supervisor in a Virginia silk mill expressed the conflict well. "I have always been afraid," she wrote, "that if laws were made discriminating for women it would work a handicap upon them." By 1923 she had changed her mind. "It would in time raise the entire standard, rather than make it hard for women."[63]

Business and professional women, organized into women's clubs and led by the Women's Party, continued to support the ERA. They were condemning, they said, not all labor laws, but laws that singled women out for special treatment. Like British feminists of an earlier age, they argued that protective legislation put women at a competitive disadvantage with men, and they urged unionization as an alternative. Their argument faltered on their refusal to acknowledge the reality of most wage-earning women's lives—a reality that underscored the movement to protect women in the labor market. Protective legislation recognized that women had two jobs, one of which had to be limited if the other were to be performed adequately. Yet legislation institutionalized the primary place of the home by denying that women were full-fledged members of the working class. In effect, protective legislation created the equivalent of a "domestic code" for working-class women. It coerced them and their employers into putting home and family ahead of women's abilities to compete for wages. At the same time, this body of legislation had little effect on those who held white-collar jobs.[64] In offices, decent conditions and shorter hours tended to prevail in any event. Legislation segregated the poorest women from their male co-workers and reduced the jobs available to them without affecting the jobs or opportunities of better-educated women such as the new office clerks.

Were protective labor laws necessary? Although most historians would agree that they succeeded in ameliorating the worst conditions under which women worked, others argue that changes in the labor force and the structure of work would have reduced hours and raised wages without the legislation.[65] Whatever its immediately useful impact, protective legislation put women into a special work category, which encouraged a division of workers along gender lines. It helped to perpetuate a stratified work force in a period when homogeneity in levels of skill might have brought male and female workers closer together.

By the early 1900s, the pattern of women's work in which most women worked at jobs open only to women had been well established. The practice of segregating women into jobs that were normally held by women was by no means rigid. A job held by males in one city might be held by females in another where the labor market was tighter, or where more opportunities presented themselves to men. But it seems to have been nearly universally true that jobs defined as women's jobs inevitably paid less than those same jobs when they were given to men. Too, women were more often paid by the piece than by the hour or the day—a practice used to keep women working hard in jobs that offered no possibility of advancement.

Streamlining Operations

Ultimately the solutions to the dilemma women faced in the work force would come from shifts in the structure of jobs— shifts that dramatically increased the number of jobs defined as female and, at the same time, improved working conditions for the work force as a whole. These shifts were rooted in the transition from a relatively competitive economy to a more economically concentrated corporate capitalism that took place between about 1890 and 1920. The creation of giant, impersonal corporations had a number of consequences for the work force. Corporations relied on bureaucratic structure and communication networks that greatly increased the demand for office workers. They encouraged streamlined methods of production, creating a managerial staff (overwhelmingly male) and introducing machinery to perform heavy production tasks. New management techniques reduced the possibility of upward mobility for male workers, making production jobs less attractive. At the same time, women could move into jobs that relied less on physical strength. These changes brought about significant increases in productivity—some of which were passed on to workers in the form of shorter hours, better working conditions, and higher wages.

The impact of this new organizational form emerges dramatically in the historical transition in office work. In 1870, the office clerk tended to be a trusted second lieutenant who handled the books and kept track of inventory. A businessman might have a personal secretary to write letters, keep appointments, and serve as confidante. Both employer and employee were likely to be male. That year, less than one percent of the women who earned wages worked as clerks, cashiers, typists, or stenographers. By 1900, 10 percent of women workers filled such jobs, and in World War I the field expanded so rapidly that by 1920 more than 25 percent of all wage-earning women worked in offices. What had happened?

dramatic shift

The developing bureaucracy required people who were fluent in English, educated enough to respond to a variety of commands efficiently, and without the need for large incomes. Initially reluctant to hire women, whose distracting influence they feared, employers succumbed to the lure of higher profits—a woman was paid about half of what a comparable man might get. One businessman explained why he preferred to hire women. Young men, he argued, wanted to be promoted and to get higher salaries as they courted girls and then began to raise families. "That kind of a clerk is not a good investment in certain jobs because for certain jobs you must have girls, as girls do not have these demands made upon them."[66]

The office walls were first breached in the labor shortage of the Civil War. From then on, it was only a matter of time before women would move into most clerical positions. When the typewriter came into general use in the 1890s, women's status was assured. The machine required nimble fingers—presumably an attribute of women. Its operators exercised no initiative. They were expected simply to copy. And the work was clean. Attracted by the new jobs, large numbers of women not previously employed began to look for jobs. These were native-born daughters of native parents, who would have found it undignified to work next to immigrant women in factories. For them, office work offered the chance to earn income without violating the domestic code.

Their entry into the labor force accompanied a transition in the structure of offices. Unlike the men they replaced, women were not hired primarily as personal secretaries. Rather, they found themselves doing tasks subdivided to produce maximal efficiency with minimal traning. A year of secretarial training could turn a woman into a competent typist and stenographer. Lesser amounts were required for file clerks, telephone operators, and bookkeepers. But it was not only her ability to perform tasks that made a woman employee attractive. Her personality was equally important. In 1916, a writer in the *Ladies' Home Journal* attributed 50 percent of the stenographer's value to her personality. Quoting an employer, he declared, "I expect from my stenographer the same service I get from the sun, with this exception: the sun often goes on a strike and it is necessary for me to use artificial light, but I pay my stenographer to work six days out of every seven and I expect her all the while to radiate my office with sunshine and sympathetic interest in the things I am trying to do."[67]

The office worker's job might have made consistent sunshine difficult. Expected to possess all the sympathetic and nurturing characteristics of a good wife, she often performed tasks as routine as those of any factory worker. Harry Braverman has pointed out that in the interests of efficiency, labor was pooled so that women would be called upon to repeat their assigned job for any number of bosses.[68] Increasingly, jobs were simplified so that tasks were reduced to the level of petty detail—a procedure justified by one office manager as fitting women who were more "temperamentally reconciled to it" than ambitious men. By the 1920s, Braverman notes, attempts to systematize and control the office led to the institution of scientific management techniques.

Frederick Taylor's notions of scientific management, introduced at the beginning of the twentieth century, offered to increase profits dramatically by creating a new cooperative framework for workers and managers. Through the use of time and motion studies, Taylor hoped to wholly control the way workers spent their time. Simultaneously, he would deprive workers of any voice in the process of production, giving that over to a managerial hierarchy entirely responsible for organizing the work process. He wanted, he said, to remove "all possible brain work" from the shop floor. Workers would be compensated for their loss of autonomy by a greater share of the higher profits reaped by dramatically improved productivity.

Taylorism was never fully applied in American industry, yet its key insight—increasing efficiency by concentrating control in managerial hands—has had widespread influence. Applied to the office, scientific management meant that the creation of office systems for filing, keeping records, and corresponding became the task of an office manager. The clerk or typist could no longer work according to her own methods, but according to methods and in the prescribed times specified by the manager. Detailed studies were to reveal optimal speeds for each task and to break down the work into its simplest components. Harry Braverman provides us with some examples drawn from a more recent business manual. The following, for example, describes the time it should take to open and close a file drawer.[69]

Open and Close	Minutes
File drawer, open and close, no selection	.040
Folder, open or close flaps	.040
Desk drawer, open side drawer of standard desk	.014
Open center drawer	.026
Close side	.015
Close center	.027
Chair activity	
Get up from chair	.033
Sit down in chair	.033
Turn in swivel chair	.009
Move in chair to adjoining desk or file (4 ft. maximum)	.050

While scientific management negated the value of skilled workers, it did not hurt the unskilled as much. Its impact on women was mixed. Women in factories benefited from the shorter hours and generally higher wages that resulted from greater productivity. Accelerating job specialization raised the demand for unskilled and semiskilled labor and increased employment opportunities for women.

But on the factory floor, pressure to perform became intense. To increase productivity, employers introduced incentive systems—extra bonuses for those who produced above their quotas. Those who could not produce were fired. Intense monotony and close supervision of repetitive tasks replaced the physical labor of an earlier period.

An expanding corporate structure relied heavily on increasing sales to sustain its growth, and retail stores began to seek large numbers of women clerks. Department store work was initially as unpleasant as any other. It required long hours, often from eight in the morning until seven or eight at night. During the Christmas season these hours were both longer and more harrowing. Even in relaxed periods, women had to stand so they would look busy. But public visibility made poor working conditions in stores easy targets for reformers' arrows. The National Consumers League urged women to boycott stores that did not offer adequate rest periods, decent lunch rooms, and seats for salesclerks. The most rudimentary conditions soon improved. To deflect further attacks and to avoid the threat of unionization, big department stores like Filene's in Boston and Bloomingdale's in New York set up welfare funds to make loans to employees in distress or to distribute turkeys at Thanksgiving. Although salesclerks earned less than either factory workers or domestic servants, many women thought their jobs desirable. Department store work had higher status because it was "cleaner" and potentially more interesting. More important, perhaps, it offered some possibility of advancement.

To meet the new needs of the labor market for people with different skill levels who could take on a variety of business and professional jobs, manufacturers supported the development of vocational schools. Initially these were privately sponsored. While young men were taught manual skills, young women were trained in the use of business machines and then placed in jobs. Companies supported secretarial schools that taught stenographic skills along with office manners. Women reformers had been urging wage earners to train for better jobs for years. In the 1890s, they organized schools for domestic servants and dressmakers. Early in the twentieth century, organizations like the Boston-based Women's Educational and Industrial Union trained department store employees in such subjects as English, arithmetic, hygiene, history of manufactured goods, art of politeness, and store diplomacy. The surge of interest in training women soon swept into the public schools. Employers began to rely on an expanding network of training programs located in the high schools to discipline young women as well as men for the work world and to endow them with necessary skills. Beginning with the first vocational training school for women in 1899 and capped by the Federal Vocational Education Act in 1917, these programs channeled suitable candidates into acceptable jobs. They preserved the dichotomy in women's two roles by insisting, in the words of one official, that young women "be trained for occupations which do not prevent development or incapacitate them for future mothers and homemakers."[70] Vocational training schools for women almost universally offered training in domestic science along with typewriting.

By the end of the 1920s, the pattern of sexual stratification had been confirmed. Most male and female workers were segregated from each other, largely by prevailing norms about proper roles, but increasingly by protective legislation and by an educational structure that reflected those norms and channeled women into jobs deemed appropriate. Within the female work force, socio-economic class influenced which women would work, as well as where they would be employed. Enticed by the image of the glamorous flapper, single women went to work in offices, department stores, and factories roughly according to education and family status. Schools and professional agencies opened their doors to those destined to become teachers, social workers, and nurses. Some women entered graduate school and became lawyers or doctors. White, native-born daughters of native-born parents dramatically increased their representation in the labor market. But married women and poor women were encouraged to remain at home unless earning money was absolutely necessary. The proportion of immigrant women and their daughters in the work force declined, as did the proportion of black women. Industrial employers, hesitant now to hire women who were protected by minimum wage and restricted hour laws, often looked elsewhere for labor. The legislative compromise that restricted but did not entirely remove female labor satisfied both employers, who had an abundance of immigrant male labor, and workingmen, who would now worry less about female competition.

But the compromise was never very effective. It began to flounder on the questions raised by women who confronted changes in their own roles at home and who, married or not, increasingly sought to earn their livings. It was finally scuttled by women's refusal to stay on the fringes of the work world they had belatedly entered. *Key attitude change*

FOUR:
Women's Social Mission

HISTORICALLY, WOMEN'S LIVES WERE BORDERED by their homes—
even where women had the leisure and the wealth to interpret
their roles broadly. The same notion of women's proper role that
limited work force options, severely regulated the lives of those
whose affluence might have made them free.

When the idea that women's sphere was to be limited by the four walls of their homes emerged early in the nineteenth century, it had both social and economic logic. Earlier, in the eighteenth century, notions of mercantile society contained a sense of the general welfare. Viewing all of society as an interdependent and organic whole, people of the eighteenth century understood the mutual responsibility of one group to another. But ideas about individualism and a competitive struggle for success eclipsed collective consciousness at the beginning of the nineteenth century. They germinated in the 1820s, taking root in the laissez faire tradition of American

103

government. In theory, laissez faire meant no special advantage
for any person or group. In practice, it opened the door to
cutthroat competition, leaving individuals unprotected by
shared social obligations. Without a sense of mutual responsibility, society placed the burden of success or failure squarely on
the shoulders of each person.

Where getting ahead was of primary importance, and where it
rested not on birth or family, but on individual effort, men had
little time for family life. To pursue the world's work, they
required well-ordered households. The women who ran them
had to take their tasks seriously and do them virtually without
support. They could not expect to seek success in this world.
Rather, they would be the instruments of male success. In
return, they could expect to receive the adoration and the
gratitude of a whole society.

While men were out seeking their daily bread, women would
make their homes havens for morality and religion. In the words
of one nineteenth-century woman, "When our husbands and
sons go forth into the busy and turbulent world, we may feel
secure that they will walk unhurt amid its snares and temptations. Their hearts will be at home, where their treasure is, and
they will rejoice to return to its sanctuary of rest, there to refresh
their wearied spirits, and renew their strength for the toils and
conflicts of life."[1] To legitimize this role, women were described
as frail and dependent creatures, physically and emotionally in
need of men's protection, but spiritually much closer to God.
What they gave up in intellectual and physical prowess, women
got back in morality and virtue. As the guardians of moral virtue,
women, in this image, were not simply to adorn their homes,
they would redeem themselves and their menfolk by unceasing
piety and purity.

Moral Reform

For every door to economic independence closed by these ideas
of women's sphere, a new door to social influence opened up.
Charged with a sense of mission, imbued with moral fervor,

many women took their commitment to virtue seriously. If they were to redeem their own men, why not all men? Single women became missionaries and went alone, or married to a partner of the church's choosing, to work among the "heathens" in China and the western territories. Married women formed associations that had a variety of benevolent purposes. Their attachment to these causes led one commentator to observe in 1841 that "Christian women have deviated from the strict line of duty in regard to their domestic responsibilities" by attaching themselves to "organized associations" instead of paying attention to their homes. A woman, observed Mrs. A.J. Graves, author of *Woman in America: Being an Examination into the Moral and Intellectual Condition of American Female Society*, could "operate far more efficiently in promoting the great interests of humanity by supervising her own household than in any other way."[2]

Many women disagreed. Those who did belonged to relatively privileged economic groups and had benefited from access to education. The Jacksonian period of American history marks the first time one can identify a sizeable group of women who had all the characteristics of the available and unpaid public servant: a sense of mission, free time, education, and a rationale for action. The period from 1830 to 1860 has been variously described as the "era of reform" or "freedom's ferment." It is no accident that women took the lead in the social upheaval of the period.

From their perspective, there was much to be done. A rapidly urbanizing society presented a host of problems. Among the worst of these were growing slums, a "degraded" factory population, rising crime rates, drunkenness, and prostitution. New transportation systems and better communication increased knowledge of other parts of the country. The issue of slavery entered public consciousness.

In addressing these problems, women defined their public roles in terms of the moral values they were charged to uphold. Christian duty led them to appeal to men on behalf of the unfortunate. They used persuasion, not force; appeals to paternalist protection, not threats. As a group, they were extraordinarily effective.

Dorothea Dix, who was born in 1802 and lived through the heart of the reform period, publicized the conditions of the insane and of prison inmates. She discovered that asylums offered cold, unventilated rooms and kept people chained like animals. Prisons, far from reforming inmates, invited them to transgress further. Juvenile facilities did not exist. Traveling the length and breadth of Massachusetts, she urged the state legislature to appropriate funds to remedy the worst conditions. Emma Willard, founder of the Troy Female Seminary in 1821; Mary Lyon, ultimately to preside over Mount Holyoke Female Seminary; and Catharine Beecher, who started her career at the Hartford Female Seminary, pioneered education for women. Though each argued for education that would train good wives and mothers, they offered women the opportunity to cultivate their intellects as well. Like Frances Wright, Scottish-born lecturer and advocate of women's education who helped to develop the community of Nashoba in Tennessee, many women participated in building utopian communities to demonstrate the possibilities of moral society.[3]

As long as women did not transcend their special sphere, their concern with social causes drew little opposition. Witness, for example, an appeal of the American Peace Society. William Ladd, its chairman until 1837, wrote a pamphlet in 1836 urging women to help put an end to war. "Political revolutions," he argued, "are brought about by men; it is not decent nor appropriate for women to embark in them. But in moral revolutions, women have a power equal, if not superior to men, and they are accountable for the use they make of it."[4] Yet Ladd urged women to employ only those methods acceptable to the Victorian world. Women were to educate their youngsters in tenderness and to discourage warlike games. They were to pray, to read peace tracts, to write peace hymns, to set up study groups on biblical attitudes toward peace. The qualities considered peculiar to women, especially suited them to work for peace. Their gentleness, their concern for humanity, and their involvement with Christianity were to be turned to the purposes of the American Peace Society.

Many women who became involved in these issues found it difficult simultaneously to accept their responsibility for guard-

ing moral values and to recognize their own limited power to
seek social change. The relentless illogic of their circumstances
forced large numbers of women from the cradle of moral reform
into the armies of the women's rights movement. Female
abolitionists frequently traversed this route, as in the case of the
Grimké sisters. The American Anti-Slavery Society eagerly
sought the help of Angelina and Sarah Grimké and others who
had worked in female anti-slavery committees. It welcomed
Angelina's cogent attacks on slavery as an institution that
separated families, destroyed marriages, and denied education to
Negroes. These issues all fell within the proper bounds of a
Christian woman's concern. And yet the society chastised her
when she used "unladylike" methods to promote these ends.

Like other female abolitionists, the Grimkés discovered that
their quest for Negro rights did not exempt them from the
boundaries of appropriate female conduct. When they began to
speak before mixed audiences of women and men, to write
letters and tracts, and to petition state and federal legislatures,
they drew attacks from people who objected to transgressions
against the boundaries of woman's proper sphere. Stunned, the
Grimkés asked how they could fight to free slaves, when they
were themselves constrained. And, like numerous other women
who had crusaded against slavery, they became feminists. "The
discussion of the rights of the slave," wrote Angelina, "has
opened the way for the discussion of other rights, and the
ultimate result will most certainly be the breaking of *every* yoke,
the letting the oppressed of every grade and description go free,
—an emancipation far more glorious than any the world has ever
yet seen...."[5]

For other women, the work of moral reform assumed urgent
proportions when it touched on prostitution. One historian has
found evidence of a small group of women who, in the 1830s and
1840s, moved directly from the discovery that huge numbers of
women earned their livelihood by prostitution, to challenging
the entire moral code that kept them there.[6] These women,
organized in the Female Moral Reform Society, raised publicly
the issue of a double standard for men and women. "Has God,"
they asked, "made a distinction in regard to the two sexes in this
respect? Is it anywhere said that what is sin in one, is not sin in

another?" Attacked by men for taking up the cause of "degraded" women, members wondered in print, why, in view of the long lists of organized female benevolence, they who wished to "unite together to take measures for the protection of our own sex," were singled out for opposition.[7]

For all their good work, the women involved in explicit social reform were never more than a small minority. In the pre-Civil War period, the social role of most women derived its strength not from what they did outside the home, but from their power within the family. And while some women took advantage of the possibilities inherent in a broad interpretation of their moral roles by representing the family in its charitable and benevolent activities, few challenged the social order in a way that transcended women's sphere.

Enlarging Women's Sphere

The Civil War and the rapid urbanization that followed it altered the limited conception of women's ability to influence the world. Large numbers of women from respectable families, eager to help their men defend the country, organized themselves into auxiliary units, the best known of which was the Sanitary Commission. Like Louisa May Alcott, the author of *Little Women*, they traveled to the front lines to nurse other people's sons and brothers. They rolled bandages, knitted socks, and arranged and catered food supplies. They ran hospitals, assisted in surgery, and helped the wounded to recuperate. When the war was over, they had learned that they could work competently, effectively, and as hard as anyone else. They could organize. And they had experienced the exhilaration of such work. Many of the women who came out of the Sanitary Commission never stopped organizing, and though most did not work for pay, they went on to apply their new self-confidence to a variety of moral reforms.

Their continuing reform work had many sparks. Some women were inspired to search for meaningful activity by what economist and social critic Thorstein Veblen called the "impulse to

purposeful action."[8] Although women whose families had acquired wealth spent some of their new leisure planning family
social life, for many, this was not enough. Enforced idleness,
servants, a decline in the birth rate, and a rigid proscription
against paid work all added up to boredom. Not uncommonly,
women developed symptoms known as neurasthenia in response. They lay abed daily, depressed and tearful, refusing to
cope with household tasks. The remedy, according to a school of
physicians headed by Dr. S. Weir Mitchell, was bed rest in a
darkened room—a cure that was sometimes worse than the
problem.[9]

Other women insisted on an education. A steady stream of
daughters from affluent and middle-class families fed the
growing numbers of coeducational universities and the new
colleges for women that opened in the 1870s and 1880s. These
women demanded, and got, challenging educations. Graduation
brought its own discontent. What were they now to do? They
had, in the common view, unfitted themselves for marriage.
More than 75 percent of the generation of college women who
graduated before 1900 remained single. Having rejected marriage, they pushed to extend their sphere of action. Yet society
made no provisions for them. Some moved hesitantly into
medical schools, attending either the few medical colleges for
women or struggling against the exclusionary policies of the
established colleges.[10] Most drifted into teaching. A few hardy
souls earned graduate degrees in economics or politics. Like the
men who had traditionally taken advantage of European universities, many fled to Europe where it was not so difficult for a
woman to complete her education.

For the most part, women, taking their cue from the Civil
War's appeal to maternal roles, transferred their injunction to do
good into a force for the nation's welfare. They would extend
charity beyond their backyards to the edges of the nation. They
would guard not only their family's morality, but that of the
country as a whole. Charlotte Perkins Gilman, herself a victim of
neurasthenia who escaped to become a leading theoretician and
an inspiration to early twentieth-century feminists, captured
the notion that women could become the "World's Mothers" in a

1903 poem. The poem, "Two Callings," begins with the sweet image of a safe, secure home:

Duty and peace and love beyond all measure!
Home! Safety! Comfort! Mother!—and I slept.

Then a bugle call—the peace was shattered, and, Gilman goes on:

I wake—I must wake! Hear—for I must hear!

The World! The World is crying! Hear its needs!
Home is a part of life—I am the whole!
Home is the cradle-stall a whole life story
Cradled in comfort through the working day?
I too am Home—the Home of all high deeds
The only Home to hold the human soul!

So when the great word "Mother" rang once more
I saw at last its meaning and its place;
Not the blind passion of the brooding past,
But Mother—the World's Mother—come at last,
To love as she had never loved before—
To feed and guard and teach the human race.

The world was full of music clear and high!
The world was full of light! The world was freer!
And I? Awake at last, in job untold,
Saw love and duty broad as life unrolled—
Wide as the earth—unbounded as the sky—
Home was the World—the World was Home to me![11]

If women could embrace the world through the most womanly of virtues, by extending helping hands and demonstrating the path of morality to the nation at large, so much the better.

For the relatively timid, this path could take a familiar route. Drawing on their prewar experience of associations, women joined together in clubs with a variety of purposes. Some described themselves as merely for entertainment, others as reading and discussion groups. But as historian Sheila Rothman has pointed out, the associations did more than hold weekly meetings. They engaged women with each other in acts of fellowship, overcoming some of the isolation of middle-class homes. They pulled them into the community, and, once there, tended to "enlarge women's sphere of interest both for self and for communal improvement."

In 1892, hundreds of small groups joined together to create the General Federation of Women's Clubs. By 1920, the federation had nearly a million members.[12] Its goals now explicitly involved community outreach. Members asked themselves what they could do to improve the social environment. Their responses ran the gamut from investigating sanitation and corruption, to raising money for worthy causes such as building hospitals, schools, or homes for the aged.

Black women had a special role to play in the club movement. Aware of the enormous problems of poverty within the black community, and excluded by discrimination from most of the white reform associations, educated black women organized themselves explicitly for community work. The National Association of Colored Women, the umbrella organization that united black women's clubs in 1896, provided guidance for local groups. Historian Gerda Lerner has provided an account of the activities of one such group—activities breath-taking in the scope of the issues they raised and clearly demonstrating that women's social activities deserved to be called work.[13] The Atlanta Neighborhood Union emerged in 1908 out of an association of faculty wives at two black colleges, Morehouse and Spelman. Concerned at first with the lack of play space for their children, the group became involved with schooling. They focused attention on raising teachers' salaries, on improving working conditions, and on getting better school facilities. They moved from these issues to health problems. They distributed literature and made home visits to encourage improved sanitation, to identify tuberculosis and other diseases, and to offer access to medical help where necessary. Sanitation was ultimately related to municipal facilities. So the women successfully agitated for better garbage removal, street drainage and paving, and home improvement. Other groups helped rural young women adjust to urban life, built hospitals and old age homes, and introduced women to the literary and cultural history of the black community.

Conditions in the growing cities offered concerned, upper-income white women their own areas for reform work. Exploding cities were filling up with immigrants from the unfamiliar cultures of southern and eastern Europe. To society's upper crust, Poles, Slovaks, and Bohemians seemed to speak strange languages and practice unfamiliar religions. Rapid urban expansion enabled a few unscrupulous individuals to take advantage of opportunities to grab money and power, using their resources to buy votes and dispense favors. City after city fell under the thumb of political bosses. Corruption and graft spread quickly, leaving morality and democratic ideals behind. Perhaps most disturbing to the middle-class observer, the nation's working people, revolting against brutally long hours and unsafe working conditions, took to the streets in a tidal wave of protest. In the 1870s and 1880s, workers, male and female, joined together in a series of protests against corporate power. Fearing a permanently divided society in which democracy itself would be engulfed, affluent women responded protectively.

A traditional charitable approach demanded care for the poor—clearly part of women's work. Yet public policy in the post-Civil War years rejected the notion of charity. Mid-nineteenth-century intellectuals had justified laissez faire government with a philosophy of social Darwinism which posited a ruthless fight to reach the top.[14] Since only the fittest could survive the struggle, social Darwinism necessarily assumed a group of unfit who would make up the "dregs" of society. The fit must refrain from overt help to the poor lest they disrupt society's natural laws, and, by making the poor dependent, deprive them of their will to struggle to the top. Women who dispensed charity within this framework were to give advice and enable poor people to help themselves. Money and food were not to be given out as they threatened to destroy character. Employment bureaus and friendly visitors would offer a helping hand only to those eager to demonstrate their own morality.

Drawing on Civil War experience of organization and administration, women who accepted this philosophy moved to reform the institutions of charity accordingly. Women like Josephine Shaw Lowell and Louisa Lee Schuyler, good friends who had worked together during the war, plunged into the work with all the self-sacrifice they had brought to the Civil War Sanitary Commission. Schuyler, a leading figure in New York State's Charities Aid Association, which she founded in 1872, undertook to bring womanly virtue to Bellevue Hospital. She turned the Charities Aid Association into a high society endeavor, involving socially prominent women in her attempt to reform the hospital's legal and administrative structure. Consistent with the social Darwinist belief that charity must "raise the character" of those to whom it was given, she helped to create Bellevue's School of Nursing. The school was designed to produce nurses of professional caliber who would provide indigent patients with models of womanly self-sacrifice.

Josephine Shaw Lowell's influence was even broader. "Charity," she argued, "must tend to raise the character and elevate the moral nature." Sheila Rothman writes that Lowell and the Charities Organization Society she directed planned to organize women, neighborhood by neighborhood, all over the nation, to visit the poor and the troubled. By listening to problems and instructing in the care of the home, they hoped "to prevent the growth of pauperism."[15]

All the virtue in the world would not solve the real problems of an immigrant population with insufficient incomes to buy food and shelter. Frances Willard and the Woman's Christian Temperance Union (WCTU) thought they had an alternative solution. With the women who devoted themsleves to charities, the leaders of the WCTU shared the sense that virtuous womanhood needed to exert its moral influence on social problems. Eight hundred thousand other women agreed. By 1920, this group, founded in 1873, had become vivid testimony to women's desire to exercise their naturally received guardianship over virtue in an active, national arena. Boldly, the WCTU proclaimed that "women will bless and brighten every place she enters, and will enter every place." To carry out their dictum required behavior that transcended popular conceptions of the "lady." WCTU members did not hesitate. The root of family problems, they argued, could be traced to alcohol. Poverty, physical abuse, child neglect, and desertion all stemmed from too much drink. Eliminate the source of family instability, and crime, prostitution, and urban filth would disappear. With all the fervor of moral crusaders, the "beloved homemakers and housekeepers" proclaimed war upon "the demon rum" and formed themselves into little armies to close down saloons. But rum was only the symbolic representative of the WCTU's underlying purpose. Leaders defined temperance as "whatever improves the social atmosphere of the home or town," and they consciously sought to extend the values of the home into the world of men.[16] In the 1920s the WCTU's goal of shutting down saloons became law for one short decade. But that is perhaps less important than the WCTU's sense of collective feminine values as an active force in achieving change.

Social Housekeeping

Morality also provided the initial root, but not the continuing impetus, for women's movements that confronted politics more directly. The social settlement is their quintessential illustration. Jane Addams, a pioneer of the movement, saw social settlements as an intersection between middle-class morality and working-class reality. Like Lillian Wald and Mary Kingsbury Simkhovitch, her colleagues in the movement, Addams hoped to bring the best of middle-class culture to the poor and, in a manner reverberating with nineteenth-century virtue, to show slum dwellers better ways to live. Demonstrating household cleanliness, nutritious food preparation, and appropriate child-rearing techniques would salvage the homes of immigrants, propping up the teetering building blocks on which the future of American democracy rested.

At the same time, Addams understood the settlement's value to a generation of young, educated women who required useful work. She wanted to create "a place for invalid girls to go and help the poor."[17] That had, after all, been her own situation. Born of an affluent Illinois family, she had suffered all the symptoms of malaise that haunted bright minds with insufficient avenues to occupation. College and an attempt at medical school heightened her desire to be useful. The tension between that desire and the limited possibilities offered by her leisured world produced a series of physical and nervous problems. Borrowing the English notion of service by settlement in the slums, Addams discovered a way of living that raised social crusades to a new level.

Like other female reformers in this period, Addams' idea for helping the poor originated out of a traditionally benevolent motive. Yet the vision of mutual benefits she brought to her settlement work loosened the moral strictness that bound the women who did charity work. Settlement workers recognized that they had something to gain as well as something to give. Perhaps that dual perception made it easier for settlement residents to see that the urban slum problems they and their neighbors faced were rooted in large societal causes. To remedy poverty they had to deal with unemployment; to promote cleanliness they had to confront discriminatory sewage systems, street paving projects, and sanitation. To elevate family life, they had to deal with work conditions that sapped energy and destroyed morale. Out of necessity, they turned from demonstrating virtue to actively participating in social and political life. No longer Lady-Bountifuls carrying their womanly virtue with them, they became what one historian has called "social housekeepers"—willing to get down on their knees to scrub the nation clean.

On a practical level this translated into activities that varied from settlement to settlement. Most conducted kindergartens that catered especially to wage-earning mothers. Many offered English language lessons, cooking classes, and lectures in nutrition. Some ran employment bureaus and offered meeting space to trade unions and clubs. Others sponsored after-school activities. Occasionally settlements were more specialized. Lillian Wald founded the first nurses settlement in New York and eventually transformed it into the Visiting Nurses Association. Church-related settlements tended to emphasize thrift. Not a few had "penny-provident" savings banks.

The role of social housekeeping, not confined to women, attracted women above all. By 1897, seventy-four settlement communities dotted the nation's oldest urban centers. About half of their best-known residents, and the large majority of young people who passed through them for periods of a few months to a few years, were women. Some of our most famous ancestors of this period began their reform work "in the settlement house": Lillian Wald, Rose Pastor Stokes, Julia Lathrop, Vida Scudder, Florence Kelley, Mary Kenney O'Sullivan—the list could go on. To these women the settlement offered homes that valued women's sensibilities and companionship, without restricting their social action. The support women offered to each other may have been essential to their ability to sustain difficult campaigns over an extended period. They drew strength and vitality from a shared sense of their place outside the mainstream.[18]

The settlement proved to be a springboard that launched women into social consciousness and encouraged them to become involved in their communities' problems. At Jane Addams' Hull House, residents, concerned about the filthy streets in their neighborhood, began to investigate the lack of city services to the poor. Their inquiries led them to uncover corruption among city aldermen and then to support reform candidates for office. They lost the political campaign, but they won a new understanding of how to achieve essential neighborhood improvements like playgrounds and regular garbage collection. Their attempts clarified the need for legislative action to remedy a host of social problems, and they began to participate actively in city and state agencies. Julia Lathrop's concern with relieving the insane and the hospitalized poor led to an unpaid but official appointment as relief investigator in the depression of 1893. So thorough were her explorations and so respected her concerns, that she was appointed to the State Board of Charities later that year. Her insistence on professional training for the staffs of state institutions made her unpopular with political appointees. But her work received wide publicity, and she was rewarded by an appointment as the paid director of the newly formed United States Children's Bureau in 1912.

Florence Kelley offers another example. Already a socialist before she went to Hull House in 1891, the settlement provided a haven from which she began to explore industrial conditions. Beginning with an investigation of tenement house labor, she agitated for legislation to restrict women's working hours and to prohibit child labor altogether. When the newly formed National Consumers League offered her the directorship in 1899, she moved to Lillian Wald's Henry Street Settlement in New York.

The social settlement idea provided single women with the possibility of mothering, without actually becoming mothers. Allen Davis, who has written a biography of Jane Addams, attributes her successful career to the paradox of having "rejected the life of wife and mother" without challenging "the conventional concept of marriage and motherhood." Descriptions of Addams sound like tributes to a parent. A professor described her life as "a sermon in self-sacrifice and a parable of service." Her image, in Davis' words, "symbolize[s] feminine benevolence, saintly devotion and practical usefulness."[19] Though Addams played the image for what it was worth, recognizing in it a path to achieving the reform she sought, she clearly did not see herself as either saintly or self-sacrificing. Clearheaded and political, she recognized that success demanded compromises, and she willingly made them. Together with other first-generation settlement workers, she opened the channels for women to move into the entire spectrum of paid and unpaid social service fields during and after World War I.

The national and state consumer leagues were logical places for women to go. Founded in 1892 by Maude Nathan and Josephine Shaw Lowell to organize the buying power of women to change the working conditions of female factory and department store workers, the National Consumers League (NCL) relied on philanthropists for support. Yet, when it hired Florence Kelley as its director in 1899, it set an unswerving professional course. Although its boards were dominated by the wealthy, the NCL's strength in big cities like New York, Chicago, and Boston rested on its ability to mobilize ordinary women not to buy products produced by sweated labor or in stores that did not treat their employees justly. Ultimately, charity turned to legislative ends. As in so many cases where morality did not block clear perception, the NCL's leaders recognized that the salvation of women and children in industry turned on a confrontation with underlying social problems. So they agitated for legislation to protect women from working under unsafe and unhealthy conditions and secured maximum hours for women in many states.

The NCL, through the auspices of its publications secretary, Josephine Goldmark, was responsible for the first major breakthrough in the field of protective legislation. Goldmark persuaded her brother-in-law Louis Brandeis to defend the concept of maximum hours before the United States Supreme Court in 1908. Goldmark did the research and wrote much of what is known as the "Brandeis Brief"—the first successful use of social evidence in American judicial history. Instead of citing legal precedent to convince the Supreme Court to uphold Oregon's law limiting the number of hours women could work, Brandeis chose to rely on the argument that overwork was socially harmful. On the basis of Goldmark's carefully amassed data, Brandeis argued that overworked women developed ulcers, varicose veins, bad work habits, and tendencies to immorality. The Court sided with Brandeis, agreeing in its decision that the "physical well-being of woman becomes an object of public interest in order to preserve the strength and vigor of the race."[20] Here was social housekeeping carried to its outer limits.

Social settlements also spawned the National Women's Trade Union league (NWTUL). Founded in 1903 by William English Walling of New York's University Settlement and Mary Kenney O'Sullivan, an ex-bookbinder, labor leader, and resident of Denison House in Boston, the NWTUL aimed to cooperate with the American Federation of Labor in helping wage-earning women to organize themselves into trade unions. The two-tiered structure of the NWTUL exemplified the greatest potential of social housekeeping. Money, political clout, and publicity came from upper-income women who were known as allies. Like Margaret Dreier Robins, for years the league's president, they used their social position, financial security, and relative leisure to fight for issues of concern to wage-earning women. But organizing strategy, strike leadership, and labor know-how came from wage-earning women, most of them single—and involved in their own union battles. Among the best known of these women were Rose Schneiderman and Pauline Newman, active in the International Ladies Garment Workers Union, who maintained lifelong bridges between the "allies" and the workers.

Both upper- and working-class women in the NWTUL justified their activity in terms of the inability of overworked and poorly paid wage-earning women to make good homes and families.

Reasoning that trade unions could provide better pay and protection against exploitation for women, they supported organizing campaigns. Around the time of the First World War, they moved to a new strategy—legislative change—to help protect and support women in the work force. They saw their attempts to forge alliances across class lines as a step beyond the traditional bounds of charity. League activities were rooted in an understanding of the necessity for social, not individual, reform, and most allies had consciously rejected charity before they ever joined the league.

In some sense the WTUL brought the transition from moral reform to social housekeeping as far as it could go. Once one accepted, as league members did, the notion that women could actively participate in changing society, the only remaining question was whether they could be paid for their work without losing status. For league members the important point was for women to join together across class lines to confront social problems. How they did so was less important than that their actions explicitly rejected the notion that women could reform others merely by demonstrating their virtue.

The Helping Professions

Accepting the social housekeepers' notion that women could participate in changing society opened up to women an array of jobs that emerged partly through their efforts. Eager to involve state and local government in ameliorating the worst of poverty's effects, and anxious to rationalize services to the disadvantaged, women in self-sustaining organizations agitated for professionalizing the social services. They wanted trained economists to analyze the wage structure under which women worked. They sought sociologists to investigate the conditions of family and work lives. They supported the creation of professional social work degrees to train women to interview and respond to clients in need of direction, and to develop social resources for aid.

In this respect, the women who fought for social reform

influenced and were part of changing moral policy in the progressive period. By the early 1900s, years of investigation, publicity, and agitation had produced a widespread sense that continuing adherence to government policies of laissez faire benefited big business at the expense of ordinary folk. Around 1900 economic concentration had reached such extremes that even a hands-off government was willing to speak out against it. To balance the scales against those who President Theodore Roosevelt called "the malefactors of great wealth," progressives sought to regulate the activities of big business. They aimed to increase economic opportunity and to create possibilities for democratic participation in government.

The progressives relied upon expertise to rescue society from the clutches of the greedy and corrupt. A well-trained class of people who could apply scientific thought to family, civic, and economic problems would point solutions to the pressing issues of the day. In a rough kind of way, expertise fell within the province of the social housekeeper. It was, after all, woman's business to point the way to a more moral and rational society. So women who became reporters, like Ida Tarbell, who exposed the corruption of the Standard Oil Company of New Jersey, could hardly be faulted on womanly grounds. And the women like Harriot Stanton Blatch, who argued for the suffrage on the grounds that women could clean up city government, had a well-established role to play.

But the real openings for women's special expertise emerged out of the progressive analysis of economic opportunity and political democracy. These essentials rested on a healthy family life. Families crippled by excessive poverty, unemployment, and brutalizing work conditions could not expect to produce contributing members of society. Investigating and correcting these evils may not have been women's exclusive domain, but doing so fell well within her province of action. Female reformers had a special role to play in shaping new legislative approaches to children and women in the family. Many of the new jobs that emerged from progressive concerns went to women who had already demonstrated proficiency as volunteers in areas where men had scarcely stepped. Jobs as factory inspectors, child labor investigators, visiting nurses, and truant officers; jobs in bureaus of labor statistics and in the personnel offices of large industries opened to women as part of their social role.

The shift in thought that subjected social policy issues to the test of expertise had broader implications for women. To do good required training first. In a strange twist of fate, women, whose earthly mission was still defined in terms of protecting virtue and preserving morality, now found a justification for access to colleges, graduate programs, medical colleges, and law schools. In the period from 1890 to the First World War—the height of the progressive period—the number of women who sought professional training multiplied. Although three quarters of the new professionals became teachers and nurses, the numbers in traditional professions like law, medicine, and science climbed, reaching their peaks around 1910. In medicine, where women had never been welcomed, even prestigious medical schools began to accept female students in the 1890s. Paradoxically, women's medical colleges, painstakingly nurtured in an earlier period when women were excluded from most medical schools, closed their doors in response to what seemed like victory. Then the newly coeducational institutions set admissions quotas for women, allowing them to constitute only 5 percent of any class. Women had won the battle for admission, but they had lost that round of the war for equality.

Access to professional training in work considered socially useful opened other doors too. Business and management courses, even banking, became legitimate as long as they were rooted in virtue and not in ambition. Elaborate justification rationalized women's entry into professional fields. Elizabeth Kemper Adams published a volume entitled *Women Professional Workers* in 1921. Part of the Chautauqua home reading series, the book was intended to describe women's new opportunities and to justify them to a rural traditional audience. Adams argued that women belonged in all professions because professionals sold "experience, judgement, and advice." They were "not working for profits." Rather, they could be viewed as "agencies of social regulation and improvement." Professional workers therefore had no "personal or partisan ends" but were, rather, motivated by "intellectual and moral devotion."[21] De-

(text continued on page 124)

Working
to Reform
the
World

The notion that
emerged in
the late nineteenth
century of women
as guardians of
moral virtue
in the home was
easily translated,
by some, into
a social mission
to reform the world.
Women worked
to alleviate many
of the problems
of a rapidly
urbanizing society,
attempting to
improve conditions
in neighborhoods,
work places,
hospitals, and
prisons. They fought
against slavery
and for world
peace. They joined
unions, started
settlement houses,
and entered the
"helping" professions.
Left: women
striking for
the right to bargain
collectively.
Top right: type-
writing class, Emma
Ransom House,
Harlem, New York,
1920s. Bottom right:
visiting nurse,
New York City, 1910.

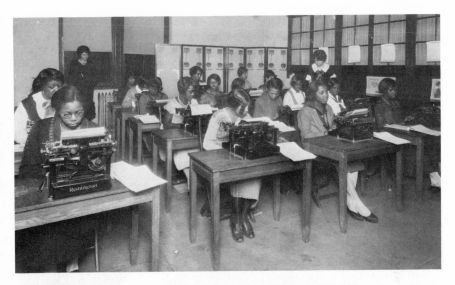

fined that way, professional jobs took on the luster of women's assigned task. As in the search for moral reform, women would bring "a free, resourceful, and unhampered intelligence" to social problems.

Translated into the reality of jobs, Adams cited the special opportunities women could find in nearly every profession. Acknowledging the value of a comfortable income, Adams noted how readily women could do good. In law, "their relative detachment from vested interests and large property transactions [left] them free to devote themselves to the human and preventive side...." They were "of course especially needed in matters concerning the protection and welfare of women and of children...in legal aid societies...as judges in juvenile courts, municipal work, courts of domestic relations, small claims court, and so on." Medicine offered "widening and increasingly varied opportunities for women, especially in connection with promotion of the health of children, of girls and women in industry, of the community, of the home." Personnel service, a growing job category for women in the second decade of the twentieth century, made particular use of women of "resourcefulness and determination. It has to do with the promotion of satisfactory human relations, the adjustment of difficulties and grievances, and the maintenance of proper standards of working and living—matters with which women are supposed to be especially qualified to deal." Adams passed lightly over banking, insurance, and management, noting that opportunities were opening, but apparently unable to specify how women could use their particular talents in these fields.[22]

World War I, with its panoply of social agencies and shortages of men, enabled women to find paid work in all the professional areas. It finally destroyed remaining myths that women lacked the physical stamina or intellectual prowess for the most demanding jobs. By 1920 a cadre of trained and eager women had carved out a series of professional areas, many of which would be loosely construed as nurturing. Most women, even professional women, still found themselves in job categories that were heavily female. Social work and welfare work employed some 20,000 people by 1920. Nearly two thirds of them were women, and that proportion was to rise. Nursing, over 90 percent female, had become a solid profession. In 1920 more than 1,700 schools were training nurses, and they had already produced more than 144,000 graduates. In less prestigious medical fields like physiotherapy and dental hygiene, women made up one half or more of the workers. And women were the backbone of all the non-supervisory aspects of education and library work.

As these areas expanded, women's opportunities increased enormously. If the statistics demonstrated an improvement in the structure of job opportunities, they also indicated what was happening to women's capacity to help each other. The professionalization of such fields as medicine and social work led to tight control by professional associations with vested interests in regulating access to and standards within the professions. The result was to threaten women's capacity to provide free or relatively inexpensive services to each other.

Midwifery is a case in point. The typical birth attendants in the early nineteenth century, midwives were pushed aside and derogated by the rising medical profession in mid-century. Yet midwifery persisted into the twentieth century as an important and valued service among immigrant and poor women who preferred to be attended by other women. When the American Medical Association consolidated its control of hospitals and state licensing in the early part of the twentieth century, midwifery was virtually abolished. Women won a few scattered places in medical schools but lost control over an essential area of health care.[23]

Nothing quite as dramatic happened when social work was professionalized. Yet there, as with library work and teaching, administration and control were removed from the hands of largely female practitioners to become the nearly exclusive preserve of male bureaucrats. Women were entering the professions—but the professions remained largely gender-divided.

Women as Housewives

Movement into the "helping" professions provided a way for educated women to enter the mainstream of national affairs. Most women took up their careers before marriage. Most, but

not all, of these daughters of the middle class retired gracefully
thereafter. Those who remained were still exceptional. Social
roles had altered enough to conceive of paid work as just barely
possible for respectable married women as long as they were
childless. Witness the 1923 newspaper headline that screamed,
"WOMAN PRESIDENT OF BANK DOES HOUSEWORK IN HER OWN HOME."[24]
But the notion that motherhood and career were compatible was
still utterly foreign. Most of his contemporaries would have
agreed with psychologist John Watson, who wrote in 1927, "The
having of children is almost an insuperable barrier to a career."[25]

Yet the same door that opened work opportunities for women
pointed the way to ambition and achievement. And as the notion
that a woman could be ambitious for herself crept into her
consciousness, it created a tension between marriage and career
new to most American women. For the unmarried, ambition
provided outlets for energy and activity that acceptably replaced
home life. For the married woman who had once had a career,
setting it aside proved to be difficult.

In the 1920s, only a few brave women tried to have both
children and a career. Among them were the "New" women of
Greenwich Village who, like Crystal Eastman, held down full-
time jobs while they struggled to maintain households. Edith
Clark wrote about her struggle in small-town America. A social
worker after college and in the early years of her marriage, she
had given up her job when her husband moved to Illinois. Three
small children and one freelance writing job later, she discovered
that without domestic help, writing without interruption for
more than fifteen minutes was a rare luxury. Resisting community pressure to participate in bake sales and civic projects
required her to withdraw into "a frigid little zone of silence."
"Yet," she concluded, "housework as a life job bores and enrages
me. Writing, even such hack work as I do, lights up windows for
my soul."[26]

Most women still worked only in their own homes. In 1920,
the census reported 9 percent of married women with husbands
present in the wage labor force. And the overwhelming majority
of them worked because of financial need. Though the numbers
of married women at wage work climbed steadily in the next few

What's the connection be alluded to?

decades, the majority remained at home. But in March 1979, the United States Bureau of Labor Statistics reported that 49.6 percent of married women with husbands present were in the labor force. At the same time, more than half of all mothers of children under eighteen were working for wages.[27]

The steady pressure among married women toward paid employment vied with traditional notions of women's work. To some extent, women who worked at home found their social tasks reduced by the professionalization of social science in the 1920s and after. Psychiatrists, nurses, old age homes, and early childhood education centers took over many of women's traditional tasks. Vocational counselors, school counselors, and marriage counselors dispensed guidance and expertise. Services formerly provided by churches and neighborhood groups were increasingly organized by paid social workers. Yet the argument that family cohesion rested on women's shoulders continued. And as women's social tasks diminished in number, the chorus of insistence that she remain inside her home grew louder. Those who did not derive personal satisfaction from lives of sacrifice were labeled masculine.

The clash of ideology and reality diminished temporarily in the depression of the 1930s. For many women, reduced incomes meant less money for recreation and more necessary activity in the home. Women increased their services to household members, making up for lost income by substituting their own labor for the goods and services they had previously purchased. Activities like sewing at home, preserving fruits, and canning vegetables increased.[28] Many families, beset by economic difficulties, turned gratefully to outside experts for aid. When the war came in 1939, family income rose, and women faced a new sort of pressure. Mothers took over the parenting and income-generating activities of fathers in the armed forces. As public antagonism against wage work retreated temporarily, women discovered a network of support systems to help reconcile jobs and family life. Those who did not undertake wage work found themselves much in demand to support community activities depleted of men. They volunteered to replace drafted teachers and served in civil defense auxiliaries.

The end of the war produced another crisis. A newly affluent society renewed its pressure on women to stay in their homes. Still focused on the disintegrating family, and fearful that there would not be enough jobs for men, the postwar period pulled all the stops out. If a woman expressed disinterest in working in the home, she was labeled psychically maladjusted, unpatriotic, antimale, and "feminist." In the words of one commentator, women had "moved...into a blind alley, dragging all sanity with them through their tremendous influence on their children."[29]

The solution was to restore the home to its place of glory. Ferdinand Lundberg and Marynia Farnham, the authors of a widely read book on women's changing roles, candidly argued that the first "task would unquestionably be one of propaganda, with a view to restoring women's sense of prestige, self-esteem as women, actual or potential mothers." Propaganda would correct "misconceptions about the nature, needs and capacities of women." And it would be reinforced by procuring "solid public honors" for "women who had raised children who turned out to be well-rounded citizens, valuable community leaders." Lundberg and Farnham rejected the notion that work at home had necessarily lessened. They argued instead that women should resist technological changes that reduced work at home on the grounds that it lowered the quality of home life. Like good crafts workers, they should uphold the quality of home-processed foods and home-baked breads. Creative approaches to their tasks would increase self-respect, with the result that women would have a "higher role than they have at present as full-time slaveys in steam laundries, canning factories, and so forth." Women, they concluded, "should obtain status and prestige through motherhood.... The emphasis of prestige, honor, subsidy and public respect should be shifted emphatically to those women recognized as serving society most fully as women."[30]

What propaganda and public policy did not do, job discrimination and housing patterns helped to accomplish. The postwar movement of families into private homes in suburban communities locked women into tight little worlds. Lacking domestic help or nearby families, they had little choice but to focus attention and aspiration on their households.

The existence of a dependable group of unpaid adult workers offered tangible advantages to their families and to the society at large. In fact, the suburban life style characteristic of America after World War II would hardly have been possible without the availability and flexibility of women who had no paid jobs. At home, women became what economist John Kenneth Galbraith has called "crypto-servants." Well off or poor, well educated or high school dropouts, most housewives did almost all their own scrubbing, laundering, marketing, and cleaning.

At the same time, wives of the business class and above performed the social functions essential to their mates' ability to rise. Short of the wealth that permitted servants, an increasingly privatized home put the housewife in the position of living almost entirely through her husband. Ironically, this happened more in affluent suburbs—where distance and space separated women from each other—than in urban working-class areas, where women, and sometimes their families, still formed communities. Well-educated and relatively affluent wives derived importance from their auxiliary roles. A researcher who asked housewives whether they had "a great deal of influence" on their husband's jobs discovered that wives tended to reply positively if their husbands were businessmen or professionals. One wife responded to a question about her importance saying, "My husband knows I'll always say and do the right thing, make the right impression." Another reported that she "was interviewed when he took the job; big companies do that." Some women believed they were responsible for "pushing" their husbands. Those who were more concerned with security and home life tended to hold husbands back, instead of encouraging them to take better jobs. This vicarious influence appeared to concern working-class women far less. Many of these women did not believe they had any influence at all over their husbands' jobs. Nor did they want any.[31]

Although suburban women focused much energy on their individual households and families, they did not do so in total isolation. They relied heavily on other women. In her novel, *The Woman's Room*, Marilyn French describes the informal visiting and the aid women provided each other. Exchanging baby-sitting, caring for the ill and the aged, car-pooling, sharing shopping, even covering up serious problems like alcoholism filled the gap between individual resources and reliance on paid or formal help from agencies. The existence of a substantial group of women with flexible schedules permitted maximum availability for emergencies.

Women within these communities created their own social networks to provide support systems for which the community would not tax itself. Unlike the charity workers of yore who had served the society's unfortunate, post-World War II housewives volunteered to participate in activities that benefited their neighbors and themselves. They became school crossing guards, PTA heads, girl scout leaders, hospital aides, museum guides, and fund-raisers for churches. Some estimates indicate that by 1965, 22 million women—three fourths of them married—served as volunteers. Together they produced around $14 billion worth of unpaid services.[32]

Just as in an earlier period when women who distributed charity had sought and won a voice in how charity was dispensed, so now the unpaid labor of volunteers turned itself into a power to be reckoned with. Parent-teacher groups, heavily female in composition, supported libraries, influenced school policies, and pressed local governments for financial support. Schools became the focal point of battles in the 1960s. Community-based groups began to demand increasing social services for children, the aged, and the disadvantaged. Organized into formal associations, women began to reactivate their contacts in churches, community halls, and social clubs to demand access to better services for their communities.

Women had engaged in political activity at least since the early 1800s. When suffrage was achieved in 1919, they organized themselves into influential but unpaid workers. The League of Women Voters rated the qualifications of candidates and advised about how to vote. Mary Dewson retired from her paid job on the Massachusetts Minimum Wage Commission to become an unpaid organizer for the national Democratic party, pulling the votes of women behind a variety of legislative acts.[33] Although by the 1960s much of women's political power had deteriorated to the level of envelope-licking and leafletting,

volunteers would not work under these conditions for long. As
in the past, they slowly demanded policy-making positions, this
time running for office in larger and larger numbers.

As wage work for women has become not only acceptable but
desirable, the contradictions inherent in volunteer work have
become apparent. Its opponents argue that traditional justifi-
cations for unpaid labor no longer apply. Society can now afford
to provide necessary social services out of the public treasury.
Shorter hours, higher wages, humanized work conditions, and
on-the-job personnel officers satisfy the need for industrial
social work. Professional social workers take up the slack among
those not employed. And community agencies have replaced the
families that once cared for orphans, the sick, and the aged. Some
proponents of women's liberation believe that volunteer work
exploits the unpaid time of housewives, reducing the pressure
they might otherwise exert on employers to restructure jobs in
ways that will permit fulfilling employment.

Others, however, see an increased need for women's volunteer
activities, not merely to provide necessary services, but to
preserve the nurturing qualities and community involvement
that might otherwise die. Herta Loeser, volunteer director of a
clearinghouse for Boston volunteers, argues that for women who
are uncertain about what kinds of careers they want, for those
who need a gradual transition from housewifery to paid work,
and for those who work at unsatisfying jobs, volunteering
provides satisfaction and education. Since leisure is no longer
the sole prerogative of the rich, she sees a potential for spreading
the idea of volunteer work to people of all socioeconomic
groups.[34] This view encourages women to continue volunteer
services despite, and because of, their ambiguous relationship to
the world of paid work.

But the complex issue of whether volunteer work reduces
pressure on government to pay for necessary services, and
therefore deprives needy people of jobs, remains unexplored.
This issue has reached the boiling point in some communities
where underfunded hospitals rely heavily on volunteer hospital
aides, often young girls. This undercuts the wages of paid
practical nurses and at the same time reduces pressure on the
community to fund hospitals at levels that will enable them to

support themselves. Such a situation results in antagonism between paid hospital workers and those who volunteer, who are almost always economically better off.

Women as Consumers

Whether involved in wage labor, in volunteer work, or simply in their own housework, nearly all women have performed the essential work of consumption. Ever since the 1880s, social critics like Thorstein Veblen have commented on women's function as the showcases of wealth. In well-to-do households, Veblen noted, women exhibited the wealth of the master. "Conspicuous consumption" in household furnishings and in women's dress and adornments reflected the ability of the husband/father to provide for his family. Elegant and restrictive women's dress that "hampers the wearer at every turn and incapacitates her for all useful exertion" revealed her utter dependence on her provider.[35]

In poorer families women served not so much as reflections of their husbands' incomes, as the guardians of it. In the extended middle classes, where women read magazines like the *Ladies' Home Journal*, they were taught how to consume wisely, stretching incomes to cover household necessities. Edward Bok, for thirty years the editor of the *Ladies' Home Journal*, undertook to educate his readers about the economics of nutritional food. Like other magazines to follow, the *Ladies' Home Journal* dispensed practical advice to women who were expected to spend their husband's money. Magazines were not above using wartime emergencies to build sales by appealing to patriotic consumers. "The *Journal*," wrote Bok as the United States entered the First World War, "will forcast the economic problems that will face the homekeeper and the mother, and show the way out...more strongly than ever will the note of actual help permeate the pages of the magazine." Bok interpreted the *Ladies' Home Journal*'s wartime mission as helping the government to conserve scarce resources and to control inflation. Monthly, the *Journal* urged its readers to curb wasteful food consumption. "To lose the war because we were unwilling to make the necessary efforts and the required sacrifices in regard to the food supply would be one of the most humiliating spectacles in history."[36]

Shortly after the war, business discovered women's role in buying. Suddenly in the 1920s, advertising, seeking to locate the markets created by newly electrified and relatively prosperous households, targeted in on women. Four out of every five sales was decided by a woman. Women made 82 percent of department store purchases and more than 81 percent of those made in grocery stores. They bought 75 percent of the pianos, 75 percent of men's socks, 90 percent of jewelry, 80 percent of electrical supplies, and more than 40 percent of automobiles. They spent more on clothes than any other member of the family.[37]

If women's magazines remained interested in serving the wife, their advertisers focused on selling products to her. Insidiously, the notion that consuming wisely equaled good mothering or good housekeeping spread from advertising pages into the content of magazines, movies, and radio. The new vacuum cleaner or toaster in the advertisement promised leisure time that would turn women into the interesting and glamorous heroines of stories and soap operas. Investing in a washing machine forestalled the ever-present threat of a husband running off from a weary wife. By the 1950s, consumption and self-image—what one bought and what one was—were inextricably bound together in a self-reinforcing cycle, making women's work and the art of being a woman one and the same.

The task of buying was more difficult when pressures on income were great. Housewives who had little income and who nevertheless had to "administer consumption," to use a phrase of economist John Kenneth Galbraith's, needed to make judgments about prices and value in the face of pressure from advertisers for specific products. It had been easier to separate real needs from imposed needs before the mass media penetrated so deeply. Whole communities then shared in pricing and buying decisions. In 1902, for example, Jewish immigrant women on New York's Lower East Side protested the rising prices of kosher meat by organizing a boycott against butcher shops. They enforced their will by dragging meat into the streets, harassing women who tried to enter the shops, and enlisting the aid of rabbis against outrageous prices. In 1905 and 1906, women led rent strikes on the Lower East Side, forcing landlords to rescind rent increases. These women have their contemporary counterparts in those who formed buying cooperatives in the early 1970s to take advantage of wholesale prices by collective purchases.

Glorifying women's home roles did not ensure that women would be content with them. The consumer role served the needs of a thriving economy—the economy would cease to grow if women ceased to buy. But women did not necessarily find the role comfortable. As firmly as the media, schools, and women themselves tried to present home roles as the only natural choices for females, women nevertheless quietly and persistently left their homes for the big world outside. Why, if the ideology were correct, would they do so? Betty Friedan exploded this myth in 1963 in her book *The Feminine Mystique*. Calling it the "problem that had no name" she put her finger on the malaise that troubled middle-class American housewives. They were simultaneously bored and overworked. They had too much to do that was tiresome and routine; too little to do that challenged their minds. If they romanticized their attractive houses and their husbands as the commercial radio did, they found them in the end insufficient. Depression, alcoholism, and sexual dissatisfaction pervaded their lives. Tranquilizers ranged from pills to bridge, golf, and sleep.[38]

Friedan touched a raw nerve. The throbbing pain, suppressed for years by individuals, became the subject of shared discussion and, for the first time since the 1920s, open to solutions. To be sure, not all women shared the pain. Some responded angrily or defensively. Poor women, women who financial necessity had pushed into wage work, single parents, widows without support—many of these people would have longed for the suburban comfort that affluent women so easily despised. In working-class families, where husbands struggled to support wives who juggled mortgage and car payments, women thought of wage work as an occasional necessity to meet economic emergencies. Even among the economically secure, many women honestly feared that leisured life styles could easily be upset by challenges to women's home-bound prerogatives. Some of these women joined groups like "Total Woman" or "Fascinating Womanhood" where they were reassured that their most important job still was ministering to the comforts of husband and children.

But among the suburban and urban affluent, and increasingly among a great variety of women from all economic environments, the ideas of the "feminine mystique" resonated. Like a dull toothache, they persisted, pervading every aspect of life until they emerged in muted rebellion. Women returned to school, worked in part-time jobs, or challenged the household division of labor. Young women stayed in school, put off marriage, refused to have children, and fought for promotions. Inevitably, as women increasingly encountered new economic and personal opportunities outside the home, family tensions increased. Husbands and wives reassessed and reevaluated their roles. The divorce rate climbed. One element of the women's liberation movement of the late sixties and early seventies was born. It joined a second element, made up of women who, in struggling for black civil rights in the voter registration campaigns and sit-ins of the early and mid-1960s, recognized that they were treated as second-class citizens by men in the movement. These young, idealistic, and courageous women quickly understood the contradiction between their involvement in the fight for black civil rights and their own distinctly secondary treatment in the movement.[39] Coming from very different directions, women who had accepted prescribed roles now sought to transcend them. To do that, they would have to shatter widely held assumptions about the home, motherhood, and sex roles. They would have to pierce the fabric of the home with the needle that would bind it, and them, to the job market. And as they did so, they would ultimately have to consider how they would work. Would it be possible for women's nurturing values to enter the work place and there influence, if not replace, the competitive and aggressive behavior of the business sector? In an extension of women's obligation to extend their virtue to the "world," women would be called upon to extend it into the bastion of male values—the marketplace. But could women successfully compete in this sector if they maintained the caring and self-sacrificing posture that has historically been defined as feminine? If women gave these up for success in the world, would they lose their nurturing qualities as well?

FIVE:

Changing the Shape
of the Work Force

FROM THE 1920s TO THE 1960s, the pattern of women's work force participation remained substantially the same. Although the numbers of women engaged in paid labor increased dramatically,

and wives, mothers, and older women worked for wages in the sixties, the jobs open to women continued to be obstinately sex-segregated. Neither war nor depression had altered the way the labor force was structured, nor shaken myths about women's proper place. Could the women's movement really offer new answers in the 1970s?

Perhaps so. The movement was rooted in a different set of realities than any of the earlier waves of feminist consciousness. Nineteenth-century feminists, who struggled for the vote and for an acknowledgment of woman's capacity to regulate her own affairs, had rarely participated in the paid labor force. By the

ATTENTION CONSUMERS:
PLEASE DON'T BUY
INJUSTICE!

ENTION CONSUMERS:
IEW YORK CITY
AL LABOR COUNCIL AFL-CIO

DON'T BUY

137

early twentieth century, organized feminists had turned this distinctive characteristic into a strength, asserting their right to a voice in public life precisely because women had special moral values associated with the home. Half a century later, a new generation of feminists turned the old arguments upside down. Rooted, in the seventies, in the labor force, they called for a legal and institutional framework that acknowledged their economic equality. They wanted access to all the perquisites of economic life. Their arguments and their power stemmed from four decades of extraordinary change in women's family and work lives. Depression and war had long stifled questions about the implications of these changes. When the questions finally emerged in the late sixties, they leaped like a traveling fuse from issue to issue, exploding the core rationalizations around which many women had built their lives.

Depression and War

After the affluence of the 1920s gave way to the depression of the 1930s, it was widely predicted that women would have to give up their jobs to make way for married men. Magazine articles in the early depression years urged women to return to their homes. No less a person than Eleanor Roosevelt declared herself in favor of affluent women volunteering their labor.[1]

Married women were especially vulnerable. Why should some families have two wage earners while others starved or went on relief for lack of work? In 1930 and 1931, some municipalities began to pressure married women into leaving their jobs. In 1932, a federal executive order decreed that only one spouse could work for the federal government, and thousands of women gave up their jobs. School boards, which had cautiously begun to hire married women in the 1920s, unilaterally fired married teachers who were women. And some companies dismissed women when they married.[2]

A few individual voices objected to these policies. Some married women who wanted to keep their jobs filed for divorce and continued to live in "sin." In one instance, women collectively threw their divorce papers at a Texas railroad company board that wanted to fire them for being married.[3] They were fired anyway. Occasionally, husbands resigned to save the jobs of better-paid wives. But the absence of collective or organized protest revealed a widespread public consensus. In the face of economic disaster, married women had no right to wage work. They could be sustained by, and in turn sustain, their families in other ways.

For a while it looked as if the pressure might succeed in pushing some women out of the labor force. As unemployment mounted to ten million people in 1931, then thirteen million in 1932—a figure that equaled one out of every four potential wage workers—unemployment among women climbed even higher. In the early years of the depression, women lost their jobs and stayed unemployed at almost double the rate of men. Then as industry shook down and selectively and slowly started to pull itself together, women were rehired at faster and faster rates. By 1936, while the general unemployment rate still hovered around 20 percent, only about 10 percent of women workers reported themselves unemployed. Their gains were mixed. Many of the jobs women moved into reflected compromises they had made to get any work at all.[4]

Yet the overall data indicate that the depression left women in a slightly better position than they had been in earlier. When figures from the census of 1940 are compared with those from 1930, they reveal some startling facts. The proportion of women among all workers climbed slightly. By 1940, more than a quarter of the nation's workers were women. Even more important, the proportion of wage-earning women who were married had leaped from less than 29 percent in 1930 to 35.5 percent in 1940. Far from driving married women out of the labor market, the depression seemed to have pulled them into it. Despite public policy, as women weighed their families' needs for earned income against the contributions they could make by staying at home, many chose to work for pay. When a husband was unemployed or underemployed, a family's need for income increased. During the depression women postponed children or had fewer of them, and so were freer to take jobs. And sometimes the depression forced extended families to live in the same household, enabling a grandparent or an aunt to care for small children while a mother looked for paid work.[5]

Women's own imperatives to seek wage work would have come to nothing had there been no jobs available. Pressures to hire men notwithstanding, employers who sought workers seemed as anxious to hire women, as women were to work. Ironically, the depression, and particularly the National Industrial Recovery Act of 1933, can be held directly responsible. The depression encouraged employers to streamline their operations, to simplify work organization, and to centralize their factory and office processes in order to maximize efficiency. They could, therefore, replace expensive skilled workers with less skilled and less expensive people—or men with women. At the same time manufacturing, especially in the heavy industries, took a long time to retool and start up, postponing job opportunities for men, whose jobs were more concentrated in these areas. In contrast, to meet the human needs of the depression, the federal government poured money into the social services and education, sectors that tended to employ women. The bureaucratic machinery created by New Deal attempts at reform absorbed additional numbers of female clericals and office workers.

Theoretically the new jobs could have gone to men, and some did. In general, male workers were reluctant to consider these jobs, and employers were not anxious to hire men for them. Jobs identified as "women's" jobs had special characteristics that employers could not ignore, even temporarily, with impunity. They demanded high education and carried low pay. They required workers who would leave voluntarily after a few years without asking, in the meantime, for expensive promotions, raises, and vacation benefits. Whether women were young and unmarried with few expenses, or married and therefore theoretically dependent upon husbands for support, they could be hired for less. Office workers of all kinds—secretaries, stenographers, typists, and clerks—fell into this category. Employers who valued stability and wanted to avoid frequent retraining, as in light manufacturing and some skilled technicians jobs, preferred married women. Either way, since women's incomes were seen as merely supplemental to men's incomes, women were not expected to be ambitious in terms of promotion or militant in terms of pay. Employers who valued these characteristics in their workers learned to reserve some jobs for women.

Because of the tight stratification of the labor force into male and female sectors, men did not take over women's jobs in any large numbers during the depression. A few became librarians and some moved into teaching and social work. But by and large these gender-defined professions remained female. Men did dominate "gender-free" jobs where the sex lines had previously been unclear or divided. Women lost ground, for example, among elevator operators and janitors as well as among college professors and musicians. They gained some jobs that had been male, particularly where the job structure had changed as a result of new machinery or streamlining of operations. The proportion of female salesclerks increased, and women took a greater number of jobs in leather and glass production and in the manufacture of electrical equipment.[6]

These rigid lines came under attack in World War II when the enormous need for labor encouraged employers to look everywhere for help. Eager to take advantage of the opportunities provided by war in Europe, and desperate after Pearl Harbor to replace the men who had been drafted, employers nevertheless hired women only cautiously. In 1940 and 1941, they turned to the reservoir of unemployed men to fill available jobs. Not until 1942, and then pushed on by the Women's Bureau and organized women's groups, did employers attempt to fill many jobs with women. For a brief two-year period, women worked in shipyards, steel mills, and ammunition factories. They welded, dug ditches, and operated fork-lift trucks. And then they were unceremoniously let go.

But between 1942 and 1944 when the war dragged on and headlines in *Fortune* magazine screamed out that "The Margin Now is Woman Power," women were allowed to do men's jobs.[7] They were offered nurseries for their children, shopping facilities, hot lunches, convenient banking arrangements, and sometimes even laundry services. Hours shrank, shifts were rearranged, new machinery was developed to take the weight off "heavy" jobs. To encourage women to stay at work, factories set up special training programs and assigned personnel to help deal with family problems. In many factories the pressure for labor broke through long-established color barriers, and for the first time black women got jobs working along side white employees. At work all women faced a barrage of slogans like:

It may be only
A Broken Wire to You
But think of the plane
That may not come through.[8]

Women who did not normally work for wages took advantage of the demand and moved into new jobs, six million strong. Other women left poorly paying jobs in domestic service, laundries, and garment factories for the lucrative pay checks of munition factories.

Was it patriotism or family need that encouraged women to take jobs? More than likely it was both of these, and the chance for personal satisfaction. Women who could not fight fascism at the front gladly offered to replace drafted men. Most did so uncomplainingly, putting up with long hours and six-day weeks as part of a wartime contribution. Still, large numbers of women testified to the costs involved. On the job, women shipyard and steel workers faced the gauntlet of male catcalls before they proved themselves able workers. At home, they still coped with the myriad problems of child care and home maintenance. For all the variety of industry and government programs, many women had to leave their children alone in locked apartments and cars in order to work. Large numbers of women coped, for the first time, with what would soon be known as the "double burden." A *New York Times* reporter asked one woman whether she was not thrilled at being part of an army of war workers. "It isn't thrilling when you're caught in a traffic jam and your children are waiting at home," she replied.[9]

The war did not alter fundamental social attitudes. Even before it ended, trade unions and the War Manpower Commission urged consideration of ways to get women to relinquish their jobs. Funding for day care ceased. Union seniority rules dictated that war workers be replaced by returning veterans. A massive propaganda campaign urged women to make room for vets. Pay checks contracted as women were demoted to less skilled jobs. The proportion of women earning wages quickly dropped to its prewar level.

Women did not seem to want to stop working. They were eased out. Seventy-five percent of those interviewed during the war years and the demobilization period overwhelmingly declared their desire to continue in their jobs. "They are the women," reporter Lucy Greenbaum observed, "who feel that if they are good enough to serve in a crisis they deserve a chance to earn a living in peacetime. They are the women who after sharing responsibilities with men during the war...will refuse to retreat to the home."[10] They were also the women who, having worked at low-paying jobs before the war, were reluctant to return to them afterwards.

Lucy Greenbaum turned out to be a good prophet. Shortly after women had been forcibly retired from the new jobs they had held during the war, they began to reappear in the labor force. But the jobs they moved into in the late forties and early fifties were not the same as the ones they had left. Women gave up jobs entirely in heavy industry, and with a few exceptions their numbers returned to the prewar level in most manufacturing industries. The proportion of female physicians and lawyers decreased. But in the expanding service sectors, women found work in ever-increasing numbers. The proportion of women who were teachers, librarians, and social workers remained at its high level. Opportunities in office work bounded upward, and the health and social service fields mushroomed.

The 1950s demonstrated what the 1920s had asserted and the depression and the war failed to dispel. "Americans," as the National Manpower Council wrote in 1957, "have not generally disapproved of women participating in paid employment." They have, however, had "and continue to have, severe reservations about married women with small children working outside the home. They have also been disposed to view with disfavor the competition which women may offer men, especially heads of families, when jobs are scarce." Public opinion data, the report continued, "indicate that Americans overwhelmingly disapprove of having the mother of young children go to work when her husband is able to support her." In short, "both men and

women take it for granted that the male is the family breadwinner and that he has a superior claim to available work,
particularly over the woman who does not have to support
herself."[11] These attitudes conditioned women's perceptions of
their labor market roles. They encouraged schools to limit
educational opportunities for women, and they underlined
public policies that continued to "protect" women against
hazardous or "inappropriate" jobs.

Contemporary Patterns

Social attitudes effectively limited the kinds of jobs women got.
They did not stop women—even the mothers of small children—
from slowly and quietly going to work. Briefly, in the fifties, the
birth rate soared. As soon as children were in school, mothers
looked for jobs to pay for education or to help buy bigger houses.
In the sixties, changing outlines of home and family contributed
to women's growing interest in paid work. Women born in the
1940s and 1950s could not assume, as their mothers had, either
that they would marry young or that their marriages would
provide lifetime economic support. More and more women were
remaining single into their late twenties. A declining birth rate
contributed to more continuous labor market participation. In
the mid-fifties, 25 of every 1,000 women age nineteen to forty
gave birth each year. By 1975, fewer than 15 out of 1,000 in this
age range gave birth annually. Household size dropped to an
average of 3.4 people. And for every three marriages contracted
after 1970, at least one, and probably two, would end in divorce.
More than 14 percent of all American families were headed by
women in 1978. In these families, women, many of them
handicapped by lack of training, had special incentives to seek
wage work.

   Older women felt an equal push into paid jobs. Those born in
the 1920s who had married and reared families in the forties and
fifties discovered by the sixties that their children had gone.
Unlike the generation before them, which benefited less from
the reduced demands of sophisticated household technology,
and whose life span was shorter, these women had time on their

hands. At the age of forty-five, they could reasonably expect at least twenty more years of active work and thirty more years of life. They were also expected to outlive men by seven or eight years. Since most had married older men, they could anticipate ten to fifteen years of widowhood. These women sought jobs as a way of making useful contributions while at the same time protecting themselves.

Even women with young children, intact families, and no pressing financial need discovered that they could contribute more to their households by working outside them at least part of the time. In affluent homes, the rules of marriage had changed. No longer required to be income-stretchers or producers, no longer sought after to care for aged parents or the ill, women were expected to be interesting, exciting partners who could maintain satisfying reciprocal relationships. People married for companionship. When "love" diminished or disappeared, they found new partners. To remain interesting, these women sought adventure in the world.

Another group of women were in families where the husband's income no longer seemed sufficient to support the family. A consumer society raised the level of "necessary" goods to the point where telephones, refrigerators, and automobiles were rarely optional. To pay for these things, and sometimes to contribute to educating children, women from lower-income families sought part-time employment if not full-time careers. As the rate of inflation mounted in the 1970s, and as unemployment rates hovered around 7 percent, women's wage work became insurance against inflation and against a husband's unemployment.

Employers had their own reasons for seeking female wage earners. As in the early part of the century, the rationale that women belonged at home continued to justify women's occupational segregation. Employers argued that women did not want responsibility, that they resisted transfers to better jobs if it meant disrupting families, and that they were more involved in their homes than in their jobs. Women themselves often sought part-time jobs, declared themselves unwilling to work for other women, and continued to train in traditional areas. They fitted perfectly into growing offices that needed more and more

clerks and secretaries of all descriptions. Many who expected
wage work to last only until marriage, willingly accepted jobs
with an aura of glamor in fields like publishing and advertising.
Lower wages seemed like a small sacrifice in the face of potential
romance. A society increasingly dependent on professional
services sold teaching, nursing, and social work to women by
appealing to their socially inculcated orientation to serve
others. As these sectors expanded, the number of job opportunities for women grew by leaps and bounds. In 1975, clerical
workers constituted the single largest category of women wage
earners, followed closely by food service workers (including
waitresses), teachers, salesclerks, and then other office personnel like typists and bookkeepers. Hairdressers, domestic servants, nurses, dietitians, and therapists were among the top ten
categories of women workers.

These jobs had all the familiar characteristics of women's
work. They were sex segregated: that is, they were defined as
women's work. They offered low pay—full-time women wage
earners continued to earn only about 60 percent of men's wages,
a figure that has hovered around the same level since the turn of
the century. Women had little opportunity for promotion, and
employers welcomed the relatively rapid turnover associated
with childbirth or marriage. A 1976 court case revealed that at
American Telephone and Telegraph, for example, more than 98
percent of all telephone operators and 94 percent of all clerical
workers were women, while men held 97 percent of middle-
management jobs. As late as 1978, 78 percent of the women in
the work force worked in sales, clerical, service, or factory jobs.
Only 22 percent had managerial or professional jobs. And of
these, huge numbers were concentrated in teaching and nursing.

Though nearly all women could be found in a narrow range of
occupations, minority race women faced the most dismal
picture of all. Still victimized by persistent discrimination, they
were the most heavily unemployed and poorly paid group in the
labor force. In 1973, they were three times as likely as white
women to be in domestic service, where pay was low, benefits
negligible, and unemployment endemic. However, because
white men earned significantly more than all other categories of
workers, by 1973 the gap between black and white women

workers was not as striking as the gap between black and white men workers. In 1973, black women were likely to be earning 90 percent of white women's wages; black men earned 72 percent of white men's wages.

While the patterns of women's labor market participation persisted, unchanged, the numbers of women entering the labor market soared. In 1950, only 32 percent of women over sixteen worked at paid jobs. By 1978, more than half (56 percent) of all women over sixteen worked for at least part of the year. In 1950, women made up less than 30 percent of the paid labor force. In 1977 they were 42 percent of all wage earners. While public policy remained as rigid as ever about discouraging women from working outside their homes, women seemed to be working nonetheless. More than half of all intact families had two wage earners by 1978, compared to a third with two wage earners in 1950. And in the mid-seventies, one third of the mothers of preschool-age children and one half of the mothers of school-age children had paid jobs. The proportion of wage-earning mothers had multiplied tenfold since 1940.[12]

In the late seventies, more than seven out of ten women in the work force worked full time. Their patterns of labor force participation appeared to be approaching those of men. Especially among the well educated, women no longer dropped out of the job market when they became mothers. Data on women in their twenties indicated future trends, describing women who no longer left their paid jobs at all when they had children, or left only for relatively brief periods. Over their life spans these women would spend only a decade less than comparable males in wage work.[13] Employers could no longer expect women to work temporarily. Nor could they expect women to retire significantly earlier than men.

If forty-two million women, as economist Carolyn Shaw Bell wrote, "would not go home again," they needed something more than dead-end jobs. By the early seventies, the impact of the increasing numbers of women in the labor market could not be ignored. Those who left their homes out of financial need wanted the promotions and high wages that were the normal rewards of hard work. They began to organize themselves into groups like Women Office Workers, Union Wage, and the

Coalition of Labor Union Women to fight for equal pay for equal work, clearer job definitions, and access to promotions. Women who left home out of the search for satisfaction wanted the personal fulfillment that jobs promised. They hoped to teach or do social work in "helping" settings. Instead they entered a tight job market where social services were being cut back to the point where workers could not help clients, they could only police them. And these women normally had no access to supervisory or policy-making positions. In both cases, women ran up against the barriers of the occupational ghetto and were prevented from moving into positions of power. They discovered that these barriers were rooted in notions that women belonged at home. The search for fair treatment in the work place demanded that Americans come to terms with whether women's family roles needed to be so rigidly prescribed.

Fighting Discrimination

Women's groups in the 1970s rejected the notion that women did not want better jobs, or that they preferred to stay at home. Under such slogans as the National Organization for Women's "Do-It-Now," they mobilized to assert women's rights within the work force. The Coalition of Labor Union Women, proclaiming that "a woman's place is in her union," struggled to move women into leadership positions and to raise women's concerns at the collective bargaining table. The National Women's Political Caucus supported women who wanted to run for office on feminist platforms.

Professional women, organized in caucuses, insisted that public policies which affirmed women's home roles engendered a series of psychic self-images and behavior patterns that predetermined women's inferior work force position. Their task was to uncover such social conditioning and to trace its origins. Educators tried to persuade school boards to review their textbooks to eliminate stereotypes of stay-at-home moms. Teachers pressured their colleagues into taking budding young female mathematicians seriously. In high schools and colleges all over the country, women's studies programs emerged to satisfy demands for information about sex roles past and present. Women historians rejected politically centered interpretations of the past and began to write a new history that placed women's lives at the core of social dynamics. English teachers and professors, organized in the Modern Language Association, recovered a body of neglected literature by women, raising important questions about the standard literary canon. Psychologists questioned notions of female passivity and masochism and rejected the idea that heterosexual marriage is the only healthy life adjustment. The Ad Hoc Woman Artists Committee objected to the exclusion of women from galleries and museums. Women in the media attempted to persuade television producers to offer images of women in active, independent roles.

Economists did some particularly significant work. Taking on the task of elucidating labor market structure and behavior, some challenged the idea that workers competed with each other in a "free" labor market where everyone had an equal chance for success. They argued, instead, that the labor force was stratified, and that people were relegated to particular tracks quite early in life. Only within each track, did people compete with each other. Between one track and another little competition occurred. The new theory explained how race, ethnicity, education, class, and sex handicapped otherwise qualified individuals in the search for good jobs. It described how each of these factors could regulate competition by limiting a person's access to education or by excluding her or him from the right clubs. Thus more privileged groups benefited by restricting competition from the less privileged. A Carnegie-Mellon public policy expert stated the problem succinctly in 1978. As women and minorities move into the "corners of the occupational structure from which they have been excluded in the past," he argued, "competition to move up the organizational ladder will be sharpened.... Whereas in 1975 there may have been ten workers competing for middle management positions, there will now be 13, and to this total you can probably add three women and three members of minority groups."[14]

Economists like Mary Stevenson, Barbara Bergmann, and Harriet Zellner described how women, who were excluded from all but a handful of job categories, were crowded into other fields, increasing competition and lowering wages in the "crowded" sectors. Since lower wages discouraged men from seeking work in these fields, certain occupations quickly became virtually one hundred percent female. Once this had happened, employers labeled the jobs "female" and considered them to be dead-end positions. Employees in these jobs had no access to promotions.

Some economists optimistically predicted improvement in the status of women as a result of shifts in the structure of work itself. Improvements in technology decreased the amount of physical strength needed to do most jobs, reducing the rationale for discrimination against women. At the same time, automation and bureaucratization increased corporate paper work, opening up new jobs in women's areas. But the picture had a dark side. As fast as women moved into lower-level management jobs, jobs as assistants and technical aides, they were still excluded from upper-managerial and policy-making positions.

To open these closed doors, women in groups like the National Organization for Women (NOW), Women's Equity Action League, and the National Advisory Committee on Women developed an attack designed to make the work lives of women more equitable and to break down barriers. They built on a foundation of federal legislation. The 1963 Equal Pay Act mandated equal pay for equal work. Title VII of the Civil Rights Act of 1964 prohibited sex discrimination in employment conditions. This was buttressed in 1965 by Executive Order 11246 prohibiting discrimination by federal contractors. Finally, Title IX of the Education Amendments of 1972 forbade sex discrimination against students and employees of educational institutions receiving federal financial assistance.[15]

Passing legislation did not guarantee enforcement. While theoretically the Equal Employment Opportunity Commission (EEOC) had the task of implementing these laws and the regulations they spawned, the EEOC quickly became so swamped with cases that it neglected individual complaints in favor of categories of discrimination. A series of court cases and a variety of supplementary statutes addressed the complex problems that emerged from antidiscrimination legislation. Public advertising was needed to notify potential applicants of openings that had traditionally been circulated along professional and trade union networks. Even advertising jobs openly might fail to attract women where legitimate qualifications emerged from years of apprenticeship or training. Women, therefore, sued to open training programs and to provide special incentives for women who wished to enter managerial-level jobs.

Antidiscrimination legislation was not cost free. It raised the hackles of privileged men who were not used to competing with women. And it particularly concerned union members anxious to protect hard-won seniority rights. The courts have consistently upheld the right of unions to protect their members' status even where to do so meant firing recently hired blacks and women. But some unions have attempted to seek equitable compromises between the competing principles of seniority rights and affirmative action. Instead of laying off all recently hired women with low seniority, some trade unions and employers have agreed to set aside a minimal number of jobs for women. Nevertheless, on the shop floor, tales of men threatened by women who have been admitted to their sanctuaries abound. The New York Times published an article on the male "backlash" in June of 1978. It reported cases such as that of one woman from whom union members withheld information and instruction until she wrenched her back trying to do an undoable job. In cases where employers were willing to make allowances in the jobs they assigned women, fellow union members refused to allow breaches of seniority that would permit women to avoid such tasks as the cleaning of men's toilets, for example. Trade unionists argued that changing the sequence of jobs perpetuated the time some men had to spend at menial jobs.[16]

More subtle forms of discrimination were harder to address. Public policy and private practice having to do with pregnancy and child care discouraged even trained women from struggling with labor market problems. Until 1978, most employer-sponsored health insurance plans either did not cover the medical costs of pregnancy or paid a nominal sum. A haphazard series of regulations, varying from state to state, permitted employers wide lattitude in reassignment and leave policies and in insurance coverage of pregnancy-related disabilities. Women who wished to have careers protested the absence of maternity leave

(text continued on page 154)

A Changing and Growing Labor Force

In the 1960s and 1970s, women increasingly worked outside of the home. The overwhelming majority of women in the paid labor force continued to work in "female" jobs, though a significant minority began to enter "male" occupations. With approximately half of all women—many of them mothers of small children—working outside of the home, demands for day care and other services for two-breadwinner families increased. Top left: male and female construction engineers working together. Bottom left: clerical worker in a hospital. Right: day care demonstration, New York City.

© by Bettye Lane

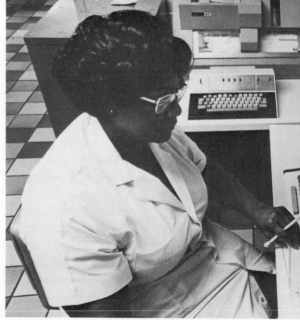

152

and demanded reinstatement without loss of seniority after giving birth. So, in 1978, women's groups joined with civil rights and labor groups to push congressional passage of a bill that prohibited discrimination on the basis of "pregnancy, childbirth or related medical conditions."[17] The law demands that employer-sponsored health plans include medical coverage for pregnancy and related disabilities and makes it illegal for employers to fire or refuse to promote women simply because they are pregnant. Although enforcement continues to be an issue, the existence of the law is an achievement.

Public policy regarding child care has been much less adequate. Since the median wage for full-time women earners in 1977 was only $8,814 (compared to $15,070 for men), most wage-earning women could not afford to pay very much either for private child care at home or for unsubsidized day care. Federal funding for child care was provided in World War II when women workers were courted. Since then it has been offered in varying amounts, usually for mothers receiving financial help under Aid to Dependent Children programs. It has effectively encouraged women who would otherwise be publicly subsidized to enter the work force. Yet when women with wage-earning spouses, on the margins of self-sufficiency, have demanded funded child care, they have been unable to get it. Public policy still emphatically rejects the notion that mothers of small children might choose to go to work. As former President Richard Nixon said when he vetoed a child-care bill in 1971, "Good public policy requires that we enhance rather than diminish both parental authority and parental involvement with children. . . . For the Federal Government to plunge headlong financially into supporting child development would commit the vast moral authority of the National Government to the side of communal approaches to child rearing over against the family centered approach."[18] Instead Congress agreed first to allow parents to deduct some portion of their child care expenses from federal taxes and then passed a "tax credit" that reimbursed working parents for a small portion of the costs of child-care.

Nixon's appraisal reflected the continuing assumption underlying all of public policy. Women's dependence on their families has been hidden in the crevices of tax legislation, old age insurance, and unemployment benefits. Social security benefits, as the *New York Times* noted in a 1979 editorial, "are still tailored to the tradition that each family has one breadwinner and that every marriage will endure."[19] The result is that the lower wage earner of a couple, nearly always the wife, often receives more benefits as a dependent than she does as an income earner. To alter the policy rationally and to give women the benefits for which they have labored would require social security to break its "traditional link to family status." Federal and state withholding taxes extract equal amounts from women's and men's paychecks and yet in many cases, when husband and wife are both employed, they pay higher taxes than two single people making the same amount of money. Such policies discourage women's full work participation.

When women workers are unemployed, they face a dual discrimination. If they are pregnant, they may be denied unemployment benefits on the ground that they are not able to take another job. Those who gave up jobs to follow their husbands' careers may not collect benefits, since they were not laid off. When it comes to retraining, women get half as many opportunities in such programs as the Comprehensive Employment Training Act (CETA) and Work Incentives (WIN) program as they should according to their proportions among the unemployed.

Women who are working face discriminatory policies that can redirect their career goals. Fewer women workers are covered by pension plans, reducing their incentive to stay at any one job or to remain continuously at work. And pension plans—which treat women as a group in determining life expectancy, despite their diverse life histories—pay women less per year than they pay men with equal contributions. Despite a 1974 law forbidding sex discrimination in granting credit, many banks still assume that women are financially dependent on families and only reluctantly issue credit to even the best-paid woman without a male countersignature.

Economic policies designed for the nation as a whole have had devastating effects on women who do not fit the dependent wife model. Inflation encourages women to seek jobs to increase their families real income. Yet it also encourages government to cut

public services of the kind that benefit women. The retrench-
ment of the mid- to late-1970s negatively affected day-care
funds, after-school programs, public sector jobs, and welfare
monies. Cutbacks in these areas particularly threatened poor
black female heads of families—51 percent of whom had
incomes below poverty levels. When President Carter's Commission on the Status of Women tried to point out the inequitable
impact on women of cuts in the social services, Bella Abzug, the
commission's chairperson, was unceremoniously fired. Policies
that increase unemployment primarily affect unskilled workers
who tend to be black and female. In the 1970s the United States
Bureau of Labor statistics discounted part of the large increase in
the rate of unemployment arguing that it was a function of
housewives seeking jobs. The United States Commission on
Civil Rights, however, took a dim view of this pronouncement. It
declared itself "deeply concerned by continuing high unemployment rates among women despite improvement in the
unemployment position of white males."[20]

In 1978, after fifteen years of affirmative action activity, large
companies reported that women filled only 10 percent of their
managerial-level positions. In colleges and universities, where
the drive for promotion and equal pay had been fought in the
courts as well as on the campus, women's relative position had
improved not one whit. The American Association of University
Women concluded, in April of 1978, that "antagonistic attitudes
within the university community" explained why women still
accounted for only 8 percent of all full professorships and 16.5
percent of all tenured slots—a gain of one half of one percent
since Title IX of the Education Amendments prohibited discrimination in 1972. Women's situation was not improving. Yet there
were some hopeful signs. Equal admissions laws encouraged
women to enter schools of law, medicine, dentistry, and business
at triple their former rate.

For the woman whose mother had worked as a domestic; who
herself worked as a hospital aide with regular hours, paid
vacations and medical benefits; and whose daughter might work
as a lab technician or a dietary aide, improvement was real
enough. But all three women occupied places in the labor force
earmarked for women, and they were therefore denied access to

the status, power, and privilege available in some men's jobs. Women benefited from the shift of the occupational structure of jobs from blue collar to white collar, but their status in the labor force relative to men remained unchanged.

To improve the relative status of women required providing access to different kinds of jobs. Economists agreed that women who were excluded by training, "old-boy networks," and experience suffered a disability. Even when training and experience were not factors, women were excluded from jobs because of deeply ingrained social attitudes. One economist, Gary Becker, after isolating all the possible reasons why men would not hire women, fell back on irrational discrimination as the only plausible explanation. Men simply did not believe women made compatible and effective co-workers and so refused to hire them even when they were qualified in all other ways.[21]

Attacking these social prejudices and the policies that ensue requires a reexamination of fundamental beliefs about the family and, specifically, about women's roles in it. To some extent, freer feelings about women undertaking wage work emerge naturally from the reality of their working lives. One study shows that in families where the wife's income was required to sustain accustomed levels of consumption, husbands encouraged wives to seek jobs and more willingly made the compromises necessary to sustain two wage-working adults. Those whose wives earned 40 percent or more of the family income were reportedly "extremely happy" their wives worked, among other reasons, because "they no longer felt obligated to stick to jobs they hated."[22]

Looking into the Future

The hard realities of economic life seem destined to encourage a continuing set of questions about household structure and women's roles. For a variety of interrelated reasons, including an inflationary economy; changes in family size and structure; the search for personal satisfaction; and new opportunities, more and more women are assuming the double burden. This puts pressure on two fronts—on the family, to adapt its style to the absence of a full-time homemaker, and on the job market, to meet the increased expectations of women. Perhaps more important, the changing pattern of women's work demands a reconciliation of the division between household work and wage work that has lasted since the industrial revolution. The combined experience of wage work and household maintenance has already begun to raise questions about some of America's basic values, including individualism, social mobility, and the possibilities for success. These questions emerge from the inescapable realities of the daily lives of women and men. They have profound implications for the future of all of us.

Look, for example, at some of the issues raised by the nature of our private households. Growing numbers of women, who are wage workers and also have primary responsibility for families, require inexpensive child care and would benefit from some form of socialized household help, like community laundries or kitchens. But an individualistic society has a hard time accommodating these needs. It rejects as marginal even those kinship networks that emerge naturally out of shared poverty.[23] Women receiving welfare aid can share it, or their services, only by putting the aid itself in jeopardy. Neither husbands nor technology help much. While relative affluence enables families to purchase washers, dryers, vacuum cleaners, and convenience foods to reduce some of the hours women are required to spend at housework, it is women who continue to do the laundry, clean the house, and prepare the meals. Despite changes in behavior patterns and expectations among a limited strata of men who have begun to participate more fully in household and child-care activities, every study through the 1970s indicated that most husbands of wage-earning women took little responsibility for household maintenance. They spent no more time than other men helping around the house. Wage-earning women continued to be responsible for housework, and if they got any help with the chores, it was generally from children. Women who went out to work reduced their standards, spent less time doing the same chores, or sacrificed leisure time.[24]

Child care poses a different kind of problem. In the 1960s many psychologists held that infants thrived if cared for by a loving adult, who did not necessarily have to be the mother. In practice the quality of day care often fell short of the most desirable. Underfunded and understaffed, day care centers fulfilled their mission haphazardly, and more than 90 percent of women who worked outside their homes resorted to makeshift child care arrangements. Inadequate government appropriations reflected widespread mistrust of socializing the most intimate tasks of mothering as well as confusion about freeing mothers for wage work. Poor conditions in some day care centers encouraged psychologists to raise questions about the potential damage to infants who experienced uneven care. Selma Fraiberg's *Every Child's Birthright: In Defense of Mothering* flatly asserted the need for maternal care and declared the alternatives either unsatisfactory or impractical. Others disagreed, arguing that the socializing advantages of day care outweighed the loss of individual attention. The smoldering controversy over the quality and quantity of day care continues, and a growing number of people are advocating community-sponsored facilities for all wage-earning mothers.

An alternative to women's double burden might be paid housework, with either partner getting a stipend for staying at home. The wages for housework movement suggests a government stipend on the grounds that people who stay in their homes to work are performing socially necessary tasks. Supporters argue that providing a wage raises the status of the home-worker and eliminates her dependence on the breadwinner. By providing an income not tied to wage labor outside the home, wages for housework might encourage men as well as women to choose home and child care roles. Yet questions about where the money would come from to support the conversion of unpaid to paid labor remain unanswered. Some opponents to wages for housework see a wage as infringing on the last place where work can be performed for personal satisfaction and not as part of a moneyed relationship. And other opponents fear that wages for housework would further reinforce the sex segregation of the work force and the privatized nature of household maintenance.

Women who face the problems presented by child care and household maintenance in a privatized home have sometimes called for collective solutions. They have suggested restructuring households on a communal basis, sharing child care among all adults; utilizing the services of the retired; and designing apartments to combine public kitchens, nurseries, and guest rooms with private space. But communal forms threaten the economic function of individual households. Our national well-being is based on mass consumption. Women's interests there-fore collide with the desire of the state to perpetuate the traditional nuclear family.

Yet the tensions of private households persist, and the unexplored possibilities of collective modes raise continuing questions about the assumption that individual family units are the "American way." Ultimately, these questions challenge the institutions that socialize us all into accepting the values of this society. Families, households, and schools quiver under the search for new roles and new ways of living. As relative affluence frees some women from spending large periods of their lives maintaining households and rearing children, it also forces them to look for alternatives. Many women develop a growing sense of the way families restrict their options. The household appears as an inefficient unit in which every woman repeats her neighbor's activity. It is experienced as confining, isolating women in trivial tasks and consumer roles and leaving many women bored and dissatisfied. Those who look to education to prepare them for employment and release from their families have discovered that women have traditionally been channeled into low-level, dead-end jobs. The social mobility promised by their high educational levels fails to materialize. Now that rationalizations about family roles can no longer explain these deprivations, some women have begun to seek creative alternatives to both traditional family life and traditional jobs.

Notions of collective responsibility in the home require more flexible working days. "Flexitime" schedules that permit indi-viduals to determine their own hours have already been tried. And reduced working hours would enable all adults to share in home care. A shift in values associated with jobs might take place with both men and women, but especially men, engaging in less competitive behavior, putting in their work days, and deriving pleasure from leisure time.

But those who oppose these concepts argue that a productive labor force rests on disciplined, competitive workers. Reducing working hours, allowing employees to exercise initiative, or shifting values would undermine the disciplinary function of work with unforeseen but possibly chaotic consequences. In addition, not everybody is sure that releasing women for the labor market is a good idea. Implicit in government data on unemployment is the assumption that women could unilaterally reduce the present high unemployment rate by staying at home. Analysts predict that economic growth in the 1980s will be considerably slower than it has been since World War II. With fewer jobs available, an influx of women wage earners will not be welcomed by many. Yet women may suffer less than men from large pockets of unemployment. Because they are likely to be hired in a sex-segregated labor market where women's jobs are increasing at a faster pace than men's jobs, they may find opportunities where men will not. This should provide an incentive to eliminate sexual segregation. Already, for example, men have moved into jobs as airline cabin attendants, telephone operators, and teachers.

Traditionally, women have taken jobs far below the levels to which their education and skills entitle them. As long as family commitment and ideas of femininity rationalized women's low place in the system of status and rewards, the inequity of their position remained hidden. But as women have begun to unmask these rationalizations, they have been able to see clearly the limited nature of social mobility. Demands for equal treatment in the job market have led to confrontations with others competing for the same jobs. In a tight job market when unemployment is high and workers are played off against each other, women begin to understand how certain workers are protected from economic ruin while others are exposed to the hazards of joblessness and the degradation of welfare.

Women's demands for good jobs have, by and large, remained unmet. This increases the numbers of people disillusioned by the promise of work and reduces the social stigmas attached to welfare, unemployment, and programs like food stamps and medicaid. Living on welfare has become acceptable to people who would have shuddered at the thought not long ago, and students are now among the largest groups of people applying for, and getting, food stamps. If a growing number of people can survive without jobs, or with only marginal work, then the value attached to work as a means of self-support is reduced. Although women are, of course, not alone responsible for raising these issues, their entry into the job market in a time of steadily diminishing employment opportunity has helped focus attention on them.

Slower economic growth, while manageable on a purely economic level, might have unforeseeable consequences. Trade unions suggest a variety of means of sharing jobs, including shorter workdays, shorter workweeks, sabbaticals for all workers, and paid educational leaves. Any of these changes would make it more feasible to combine work at home with wage work. Before she became Secretary of Commerce in 1976, Juanita Kreps suggested the notion of spreading out leisure time. Instead of forcing workers to retire at age sixty-five, she argued, they ought to be encouraged to take a paid year or two off during their work lives in order to meet family needs or to gain some education.[25] But all these alternatives beg questions about what will happen to an individual's incentive to "get ahead." Success in our labor market has historically required putting the job first and working endless hours. What would happen to this drive if everybody shared jobs or got paid leaves? Can a society based on competition and free enterprise continue to function if workers no longer value the rewards of competitive behavior?

Out of the struggle to come to grips with the transition in women's roles has come one of the most meaningful slogans of the contemporary women's movement, "the personal is political." The slogan embodies a recognition that problems women experienced as individuals often reflected larger social relations that were both the cause and condition of women's commonly shared oppression. Sexual harassment on the job, for example, reflected the general perception of women as "sex objects" who were not to be taken seriously in the world of ideas or of work. A husband who demanded service from his wife echoed society's insistence on nurturing and passive roles for women. Each woman who protested these presumably personal acts raised her voice against deeply held convictions that were themselves responsible for restricting her ability to function as an independent human being.

More powerful was the dawning recognition that these attitudes were not only held by men, but were shared by women too. Because of a complex socialization process that reinforced different kinds of behavior for males and females from birth on, women had developed characteristics that helped to perpetuate their dependent status. They were likely to have low self-esteem and to fail to aspire to succeed. One of the most significant contributions of the contemporary women's movement was the way in which it provided a clear vision of the hidden socialization process. As women have become aware of the ways that child-rearing practices, books, television, advertising, schools, and social relationships have restricted their choices, they have been better able to understand their position in the home and in the labor market. They have worked to alter some of the messages people receive about "appropriate" behavior. And with members of ethnic and racial groups, they have demanded more varied models of people in positions of authority with whom to identify. Control over black schools by black people, a resurgence of interest in women's colleges in the mid-1970s, and the rapid expansion of women's studies programs and courses in schools all over the country reflect a trend with enormous implications for altering the self-images that have sustained traditional roles. Persistent and continuous exposure of the way roles limit people's lives encourages women to exert themselves to the point of rejecting male supremacy. Resulting pressures on the media and the job market could permanently alter the discouraging pattern of women in positions of prestige and authority. They, in turn, could encourage others to try similar roles. In challenging the job structure, women are challenging the entire fabric of psychic oppression that limits aspirations and stifles creative growth. They are lifting the veil that has obscured the nature of women's lives and work, inside and outside the home.

But one veil is easily replaced by another, and women can be enticed into a competitive framework that will continue to restrict our vision of reality. A few women are already being offered desirable jobs in traditional bastions of power and prestige. For many others, it is tempting to accept the outward appearance of social mobility: new job titles and small salary increases. Women are expected to take their rewards gratefully, without challenging the prevailing power structures. At the same time they act as models for younger women to emulate. While such a process might eventually minimize distinctions between male and female jobs, it would do so by socializing women into current definitions of work without threatening male supremacy or questioning the value and belief systems that sustain an unequal distribution of power.

The analysis offered by economist Carolyn Shaw Bell, for example, accepts male definitions of work. Bell argues that women who conceive of the home as their responsibility give employers rational explanations for excluding them.[26] These women have "different criteria in job research and job selection" looking for working hours that coincide with children's school days or policies that permit vacations on the husband's schedule. They trade off money and position for the gains of shorter travel time, convenient location, or flexible schedules. They abandon jobs when husbands move. In the end, Bell argues, their contribution falls short of that offered by men. They lack the "long-term work involvement which leads to acquired skills, familiarity with routine and confidence in dealing with the unexpected, acquaintance with others in the field and with accepted and developing ways of doing business." Bell's solution to this situation is to free women from the assumption that maintaining a household is their responsibility by making the home attractive to men and simultaneously making wage work attractive to women. Compulsory child care insurance, elimination of the "dependent spouse" category on taxes and for social security purposes, a special tax on men for the care of all children, and extra-heavy taxes on male wage earners might encourage men to care for their children at home.

Though such a solution might seem attractive to women who want to "make it" in the present world, it offers little hope to those who are searching for ways of dealing equitably and humanely with home and child care while also moving toward the full participation of women and men in the labor force. An alternate response would involve adapting job structures and work related goals to reflect less concern with efficient production and more with humane values.

Fundamental solutions for the future will require creative redefinitions of both work and family. They will require new perceptions of optional work activity and imaginative approaches to new forms of the family. Some of these will be forced upon us by the harsh demands of economic life. Others will emerge in an inevitable cycle of adjustment and compromise. Exploring various alternatives will be the enormously exciting task of the next generation.

About the Author

ALICE KESSLER-HARRIS is co-director of the Hofstra University Center for the Study of Work and Leisure, a center dedicated to doing research on and creating programs for trade unions. She is an administrator and teacher in the center's education program at District 65, UAW. Kessler-Harris, who has a Ph.D. in history from Rutgers University, has received a number of grants and awards, including a National Endowment for the Humanities Fellowship and a Radcliffe Institute Fellowship. She has taught at Sarah Lawrence College, where she was director of the women's studies program, and at the Centre for the Study of Social History, at the University of Warwick in England. Alice Kessler-Harris has published articles on women and work in many journals and anthologies and is co-editor of *Past Imperfect: Alternative Essays in American History.*

A Note on Language

IN EDITING BOOKS, The Feminist Press attempts to eliminate harmful sex and race bias inherent in the language. In order to retain the authenticity of historical and literary documents, however, our policy is to leave their original language unaltered. We recognize that the task of changing language usage is extremely complex and that it will not be easily accomplished. The process is an ongoing one that we share with many others concerned with the relationship between a humane language and a more humane world.

Notes

One: The Meaning of Work in Women's Lives

1. Quoted in Ann Douglas, *The Feminization of American Culture* (New York: Alfred A. Knopf, 1977), p. 52.

2. Ivy Pinchbeck, *Women Workers and the Industrial Revolution: 1750–1850* (1930; reprint ed., New York: Augustus M. Kelley, 1969), p. 76 and chap. I, passim.

3. Edmund Morgan, "The Labor Problem of Jamestown: 1607–1618," *American Historical Review* 76 (June 1971):595–611; Sigmund Diamond, "From Organization to Society: Virginia in the Seventeenth Century," in *Colonial America: Essays in Politics and Social Development*, ed. Stanley Katz (Boston: Little, Brown and Company, 1971).

4. Julia Cherry Spruill, *Women's Life and Work in the Southern Colonies* (1938; reprint ed., New York: W.W. Norton & Co., 1972), pp. 11–14; Edith Abbott, *Women in Industry* (1910; reprint ed., New York: Arno Press, 1969), pp. 11–12.

5. Eugenia Andruss Leonard, *The Dear-Bought Heritage* (Philadelphia: University of Pennsylvania Press, 1965), pp. 204–205.

6. Douglas Jones, "The Strolling Poor: Transiency in Eighteenth-Century Massachusetts," *Journal of Social History* 8 (Spring 1975):34–35.

7. Leonard, *Dear-Bought Heritage*, p. 204.

8. Benjamin Franklin, *The Autobiography and Other Writings*, ed. L. Jesse Lemisch (New York: New American Library, 1961), p. 187.

9. Herbert Gutman, *Work, Culture and Society in Industrializing America* (New York: Alfred A. Knopf, 1976), pp. 14–15.

10. Michael Katz, *Class, Bureaucracy and Schools* (New York: Praeger Publishers, 1971), pp. 10–11.

11. Quoted in Henry May, *Protestant Churches and Industrial America* (New York: Harper Torchbooks, 1949), p. 69.

12. This position is satirized by Joe Hill, the Industrial Workers of the World song writer who wrote, in "The Preacher and the Slave":

> You will eat, bye and bye,
> In that glorious land above the sky;
> Work and pray, live on hay,
> You'll get pie in the sky when you die.

13. May, *Protestant Churches and Industrial America*, p. 94.

14. Alice S. Rossi, *The Feminist Papers* (New York: Bantam Books, 1973), pp. 251–252.

15. Pinchbeck, *Women Workers and the Industrial Revolution*, pp. 312–313.

16. Barbara Welter, "The Cult of True Womanhood: 1820–1860," *American Quarterly* 18 (Summer 1964).

17. Margaret Fuller, *Woman in the Nineteenth Century* (1855; reprint ed., New York: W.W. Norton & Co., 1971), p. 30.

18. The complete text of the poem can be found in Joyce Kornbluh, ed., *Rebel Voices: An I.W.W. Anthology* (Ann Arbor: University of Michigan Press, 1972), p. 196.

19. Gutman, *Work, Culture and Society*, p. 544.

20. *Work in America*, Report of a Special Task Force to the Secretary of Health, Education, and Welfare

(Cambridge, Mass.: M.I.T. Press, 1973), p. xix and chap. I.

Two: Household Labor

1. James T. Lemon, "Household Consumption in Eighteenth Century America and Its Relationship to Production and Trade: The Situation among Farmers in South Eastern Pennsylvania," *Agricultural History* 41 (January 1967):60. Lemon estimates that 80 percent of all farms in Southeastern Pennsylvania in the fifty years from 1740 to 1790 produced some surplus grain— perhaps as much as 40 percent of their whole crop. I am indebted to Phyllis Vine for calling this article to my attention.

2. Alice Morse Earle, *Colonial Dames and Goodwives* (Boston: Houghton, Mifflin and Co., 1895), pp. 312–313.

3. Julia Cherry Spruill, *Women's Life and Work in the Southern Colonies* (1938; reprint ed., New York: W.W. Norton & Co., 1972), p. 64.

4. Ibid., p. 65.

5. Gerda Lerner, *Black Women in White America* (New York: Pantheon Books, 1972), p. 15.

6. Quoted in Nancy Cott, ed., *Root of Bitterness: Documents of the Social History of American Women* (New York: E.P. Dutton & Co., 1972), p. 31.

7. Ibid., p. 89–90.

8. Douglas Lamar Jones, "The Strolling Poor: Transiency in Eighteenth Century Massachusetts," *Journal of Social History* 7 (Spring 1975):34. Jones argues that half of all transients were women.

9. Robert Hutchinson, ed., *Poems of Anne Bradstreet* (New York: Dover Publications, 1969), pp. 57, 58. See John Demos, *A Little*

Commonwealth: Family Life in Plymouth Colony (New York: Oxford University Press, 1970), pp. 68–69 for more demographic data.

10. Edmund Morgan, *The Puritan Family: Religion and Domestic Relations in Seventeenth Century New England* (1944; reprint ed., New York: Harper & Row, 1966), p. 76.

11. Rolla Milton Tryon, *Household Manufactures in the U.S.: 1640–1860* (Chicago: University of Chicago Press, 1917), p. 33.

12. Alan Dawley, *Class and Community: The Industrial Revolution in Lynn* (Cambridge, Mass.: Harvard University Press, 1976), p. 14.

13. Tryon, *Household Manufactures*, pp. 304–305.

14. Philip Greven, *Four Generations: Population, Land, and Family in Colonial Andover, Massachusetts* (Ithaca, N.Y.: Cornell University Press, 1970). See chapter 7 and especially page 203 for examples of children born in 1850.

15. Nancy Cott, *The Bonds of Womanhood: "Woman's Sphere" in New England, 1780–1835* (New Haven, Conn.: Yale University Press, 1977), p. 71.

16. Bernard Wishy, *The Child and the Republic* (Philadelphia: University of Pennsylvania Press, 1972), p. 28.

17. Mrs. A.J. Graves, "Women in America," in Nancy Cott, *Root of Bitterness* (New York: E.P. Dutton & Co., 1972), p. 141.

18. Gerda Lerner, *The Female Experience: An American Documentary* (Indianapolis: Bobbs-Merrill Co., 1977), p. 116.

19. Anne Firor Scott, *The Southern Lady: From Pedestal to Politics, 1830–1930* (Chicago: University of Chicago Press, 1970), pp. 33–34.

20. Catharine E. Beecher and Harriet Beecher Stowe, *The American Woman's Home: or Principles of Domestic Science* (1869; reprint ed., New York: Arno Press, 1971), p. 13.

21. Dolores Hayden, "Two Utopian Feminists and Their Campaigns for Kitchenless Houses," *Signs* 4 (Winter 1978):276. Hayden discusses the architectural influence of Pierce and Howland on such thinkers as Ralph Bellamy and Charlotte Perkins Gilman.

22. Siegfried Giedion, *Mechanization Takes Command: A Contribution to Anonymous History* (New York: W.W. Norton & Co., 1948), p. 560ff.

23. *Ladies' Home Journal,* October 1911, quoted in Barbara Ehrenreich and Deirdre English, "The Manufacture of Housework," *Socialist Review* 5 (October-December 1975):16.

24. Ibid., p. 20.

25. Julie Roy Jeffrey, "Women in the Southern Farmers' Alliance: A Reconstruction of the Role and Status of Women in the Late Nineteenth-Century South," *Feminist Studies* 3 (Fall 1975):83.

26. Margaret Jarman Hagood, *Mothers of the South: Portraiture of the White Tenant Farm Woman* (1939; reprint ed., W.W. Norton & Co., 1977), pp. 100–101.

27. John B. Andrews and W.D.P. Bliss, *History of Women in Trade Unions,* Report on the condition of women and child wage earners in the United States, vol. 10, Senate Document #645, 61st Congress, 2nd Session (1911; reprint ed., New York: Arno Press, 1974), p. 47.

28. Isaac A. Hourwich, *Immigration and Labor: The Economic Aspects of European Immigration to the United States* (New York: B.W. Huebsch, 1922), p. 232.

29. Susan J. Kleinberg, "Technology and Women's Work: The Lives of Working Class Women in Pittsburgh, 1870-1900," *Labor History* 17 (Winter 1976):61.

30. Ibid., p. 62–63.

31. Anzia Yezierska, *Arrogant Beggar* (New York: Grosset & Dunlap, 1927), p. 14.

32. Margaret Byington, *Homestead: The Households of a Mill Town* (1910; reprint ed., Pittsburgh: University of Pittsburgh Press, 1974), chap. 10, and especially pp. 152, 154.

33. Anthony F.C. Wallace, *Rockdale: The Growth of an American Village in the Early Industrial Revolution* (New York: Alfred A. Knopf, 1978), chap. II.

34. Carol Groneman, "She Earns as a Child—She Pays as a Man: Women Workers in a Mid-Nineteenth-Century New York City Community," in Richard Ehrlich ed., *Immigrants in Industrial America* (Charlottesville, Va.: University Press of Virginia, 1977), p. 39. See also Byington, *Homestead,* p. 142; and Virginia Yans, *Family and Community: Italian Immigrants in Buffalo, 1880-1930* (Ithaca, N.Y.: Cornell University Press, 1977), p. 200.

35. Isaac Metzker, ed., *A Bintel Brief* (New York: Ballantine Books, 1971), pp. 65–66.

36. Ella Wolff interview in Amerikaner Yiddishe Geshichte Bel Pe, Yivo archives, p. 3.

37. Ehrenreich and English, "The Manufacture of Housework," p. 33.

38. Robert S. Lynd and Helen Merrell Lynd, *Middletown: A Study in Modern American Culture* (New York: Harcourt, Brace and World, 1929), p. 163.

39. Joan Vanek, "Time Spent in Housework," *Scientific American* 231 (November 1974):116–120. Some more recent studies indicate that wage-earning wives now work comparatively fewer hours in the home than non-wage-earning wives. See, for example, Lawrence Van Gelder, "Time Spent on Housework Declines," *New York Times,* 22 May 1979, p. C10.

40. Quoted in Betty Friedan, *The Feminine Mystique* (New York: Dell Publishing Co., 1963), pp. 52, 53.

Three: Working for Wages

1. Edith Abbott, *Women in Industry: A Study in American Economic History (1910; reprint ed.,* New York: Arno Press, 1969), p. 40.

2. Leo Marx, *The Machine in the Garden: Technology and the Pastoral Ideal in America* (New York: Oxford University Press, 1964), p. 134.

3. Abbott, *Women in Industry,* p. 50.

4. Caroline T. Ware, *The Early New England Cotton Manufactures: A Study in Industrial Beginnings* (Boston: Houghton Mifflin Co., 1931), p. 198; Hanna Josephson, *The Golden Threads: New England's Mill Girls and Magnates* (New York: Duell, Sloan and Pearce, 1949), p. 22; Oscar Handlin, *Boston's Immigrants: 1790–1880* (1941; reprint ed., New York: Atheneum Publishers, 1971), pp. 74–76; and Reinhard Bendix, *Work and Authority in Industry: Ideologies of Management* (New York: John Wiley & Sons, 1956), p. 39.

5. Josephson, *The Golden Threads,* pp. 63, 23. See also John Kasson, *Civilizing the Machine: Technology, Aesthetics, and Republican Values in America: 1776–1900* (New York: Penguin Books, 1976), p. 70; and Holland Thompson, *From the Cotton Field to the Cotton Mill: A Study of the Industrial Transition in North Carolina* (1906; reprint ed., New York: Books for Libraries Press, 1971), p. 52 for similar examples of paternal employment in the South. About one half of the employees in the New England textile mills were recruited in this way. A small, though undetermined, number of women who worked in the mills were self-supporting and responsible for families of their own.

6. "Susan Miller," in Benita Eisler, ed., *The Lowell Offering: Writing by New England Mill Women, 1840–1845* (Philadelphia: J.B. Lippincott Co., 1977), pp. 172–183.

7. John B. Andrews and W.D.P. Bliss, *History of Women in Trade Unions,* Report on the Condition of Women and Child Wage Earners in the United States, vol. 10, Senate Document #645, 61st Congress, 2nd Session (1911; reprint ed., New York: Arno Press, 1974), p. 12. See also Thomas Dublin, *Women at Work: The Transformation of Work and Community in Lowell, Massachusetts, 1820–1860* (New York: Columbia University Press, 1979), chap. 6.

8. Andrews and Bliss, *History of Women in Trade Unions,* p. 31.

9. Ware, *The Early New England Cotton Manufactures,* p. 231. See Dublin, *Women at Work,* chap. 8 for data on this transformation in one mill.

10. Ware, *The Early New England Cotton Manufactures,* p. 234.

11. Quoted in Constance McLaughlin Green, *Holyoke, Massachusetts: A Case History of the Industrial Revolution in America* (New Haven: Yale University Press, 1939), p. 31fn.

12. Lucy Maynard Salmon, *Domestic Service* (New York: Macmillan, 1911), p. 71.

13. Aileen Kraditor, *Up From the Pedestal* (Chicago: Quadrangle, 1968), p. 13. Kraditor continues, "The home was the bulwark against social disorder, and woman was the creator of the home...she occupied a desperately necessary place as symbol and center of the one institution that prevented society from flying apart."

14. Quoted in Ruth Miller Elson, *Guardians of Tradition: American Schoolbooks of the Nineteenth Century* (Lincoln: University of Nebraska Press, 1964), p. 309.

15. Andrews and Bliss, *History of Women in Trade Unions*, p. 118.

16. See, for example, Green, *Holyoke, Massachusetts*. Helen Sumner, *History of Women in Industry in the United States*, Report on the Condition of Women and Child Wage Earners in the United States, vol. 9, Senate Document #645, 61st Congress, 2nd Session (Washington, D.C.: Government Printing Office, 1910), p. 28, reports that the *Workingman's Advocate* in 1868 complained that women only got one quarter of men's wages. Handlin, *Boston's Immigrants*, p. 81, notes that women earned an average of $1.50 to $3 per week, while men earned from $4.50 to $5.50. See also John R. Commons et al., eds., *A Documentary History of American Industrial Society*, The Labor Movement, vol. 6 (Glendale: A.H. Clark, 1910), p. 195; and Emilie Josephine Hutchinson, *Women's Wages: A Study of the Wages of Industrial Women and Measures Suggested to Increase Them* (Providence: American Mathematical Society, 1968), pp. 24, 25.

17. Commons, *A Documentary History*, pp. 282, 284.

18. Andrews and Bliss, *History of Women in Trade Unions*, p. 48.

19. Elizabeth F. Baker, *Technology and Women's Work* (New York: Columbia University Press, 1964), p. 17. See also Sumner, *History of Women in Industry*, p. 51, who indicates that the number of women teachers dropped to 40.6 percent in 1900; and Michael Katz, *The Irony of Early School Reform* (Boston: Beacon Press, 1968), p. 12.

20. Quoted in Sumner, *History of Women in Industry*, p. 29.

21. Andrews and Bliss, *History of Women in Trade Unions*, p. 104.

22. *The Silk Industry*, Report on the Conditions of Women and Child Wage Earners, vol. 4, Senate Document #645, 61st Congress, 2nd Session (Washington, D.C.: Government Printing Office, 1910), pp. 40, 41.

23. Andrews and Bliss, *History of Women in Trade Unions*, p. 122.

24. Hutchinson, *Women's Wages*, pp. 159–160; Andrews and Bliss, *History of Women in Trade Unions*, p. 151, and see p. 179 for the cigar industry. The report attributes the decline in membership that occurred among women after 1902 to deliberate hostility by employers.

25. Examples of positive and negative attitudes can be found in Andrews and Bliss, *History of Women in Trade Unions*, pp. 39, 41, 46, 47, 57; Sumner, *History of Women in Industry*, pp. 61fn.; and Commons, *A Documentary History*, p. 205.

26. *New York Daily Tribune*, 7 March 1845, p. 2.

27. *New York Daily Tribune*, 19 August 1845, p. 2.

28. William Sanger, *The History of Prostitution* (New York: The Medical Publishing Co., 1897), pp. 603–604.

29. Virginia Penny, *Think and*

Act: A Series of Articles Pertaining to Men and Women, Work and Wages (Philadelphia: Claxton, Remsen and Haffelfinger, 1869), p. iii.

30. Mary Conyngton, *Relation Between Occupation and Criminality of Women*, Report on the Condition of Women and Child Wage Earners in the United States, vol. 15, Senate Document #645, 61st Congress, 2nd Session (Washington, D.C.: Government Printing Office, 1911), p. 102.

31. U.S. Commissioner of Labor, *Working Women in Large Cities, Fourth Annual Report, 1888* (Washington, D.C.: Government Printing Office, 1889), pp. 74–75.

32. Margaret Byington, *Homestead: The Households of a Mill Town* (Pittsburgh: University of Pittsburgh Press, 1974), p. 201.

33. For example, see Louise Odencrantz, *Italian Women in Industry* (New York: Russell Sage, 1919), p. 21.

34. *Workingmen's Advocate*, 24 April 1869, p. 1.

35. Anthony Wallace, *Rockdale: The Growth of an American Village in the Early Industrial Revolution* (New York: Alfred A. Knopf, 1978), chap. 2; and Daniel Walkowitz, "Working Class Women in the Gilded Age: Factory, Community and Family Life Among Cohoes, N.Y. Cotton Factory Workers," *Journal of Social History* 5 (Summer 1972):462–90.

36. Joseph A. Hill, *Women in Gainful Occupations: 1870–1920*, Census Monograph IX (Washington, D.C.: Government Printing Office, 1929), pp. 75–76.

37. Ibid., pp. 19–20.

38. Louisa May Alcott, *Work* (New York: Schocken Books, 1977), p. 22.

39. Chart adapted from Louise Bosworth, *The Living Wage of Women Workers* (Philadelphia: The American Academy of Political and Social Science, 1911), p. 90.

40. Ibid.

41. *Independent*, 4 June 1874, p. 1. I am grateful to Sarah Elbert for sending me a copy of this article.

42. Barbara Klaczynska, "Why Women Work: A Comparison of Various Groups—Philadelphia, 1910–1930," *Labor History* 17 (Winter 1976):73–87.

43. David Katzman, *Seven Days a Week: Women and Domestic Service in Industrializing America* (New York: Oxford University Press, 1978), pp. 120–121.

44. Young Women's Christian Association, First Report of the Commission on Household Employment, May 5–11, 1915, p. 6.

45. Cambridge, Mass., Schlesinger Library, Women's Educational and Industrial Union collection, Box 1, file 9.

46. YMCA, First Report of the Commission on Household Employment, p. 19.

47. Katzman, *Seven Days a Week*, Appendix 1, especially p. 289.

48. Gerda Lerner, *Black Women in White America: A Documentary History* (New York: Pantheon Books, 1972), pp. 229–230.

49. Quoted in Sumner, *History of Women in Industry*, p. 129. See also p. 123. The *Tribune* estimated the yearly income of a seamstress as $91 in June of 1853.

50. Quoted in Sumner, *History of Women in Industry*, p. 140.

51. Mary Van Kleeck, *Women in the Bookbinding Trade* (New York: Survey Associates, 1913), p. 219.

52. Carroll D. Wright, *The Working Girls of Boston*, Fifteenth Annual Report of the Massachusetts

Bureau of the Statistics of Labor
(Boston: Wright & Potter, 1884),
pp. 69-72.

53. Charlotte Perkins Gilman,
The Home, Its Work and Influence
(1903; reprint ed.,Urbana, Ill.:
University of Illinois Press,
1972), p. 46. See also Gilman's
Woman and Economics (1898;
reprint ed., New York: Harper &
Row, 1966).

54. Blanche Wiesen Cook, ed.,
*Crystal Eastman on Women and
Revolution* (New York: Oxford
University Press, 1978), pp. 6-7.

55. Ann Craton Blankenhorn
collection, Archives of Labor and
Urban Affairs, Box 1, file 23, Chap. 2,
p. 12, Wayne State University,
Detroit.

56. Quoted in Andrews and Bliss,
History of Women in Trade Unions,
p. 173.

57. For more detailed figures and
an explanation of trade unions
exclusion of women see Alice
Kessler-Harris, "Where Are the
Organized Women Workers?"
Feminist Studies, Fall 1975, pp.
92-110.

58. Hutchinson, *Women's Wages,*
p. 81.

59. John R. Commons and John B.
Andrews, *Principles of Labor
Legislation,* rev. ed. (New York:
Harper and Brothers 1927), pp. 69,
30.

60. Women's Bureau Collection,
accession #5A101, Box 40, Bulletin
#15, Individual Interviews,
Massachusetts, National Archives,
Washington, D.C.

61. Labor force participation rate
can be found in Valerie
Oppenheimer, *The Female Labor
Force in the United States* (Berkeley:
University of California Press, 1969),
pp. 3-5; Janet M. Hooks, *Women's
Occupations through Seven Decades,*

p. 34; and William Chafe, *The
American Woman, Her Changing
Social, Political and Feminine Roles*
(New York: Oxford University Press,
1972) pp. 54-55. I have not
attempted to estimate how much
these changes were affected by
increased affluence or by the
withdrawal of immigrant women
from the labor market. For an
account of the effect of minimum
wages on the most disadvantaged
group of workers, see Elizabeth Ross
Haynes, "Two Million Women at
Work," in Gerda Lerner, *Black
Women in White America.* Writing
in 1922, Haynes notes, "With the
fixing of the minimum wage in the
hotels, restaurants, etc., at $16.50 for
a 48 hour week, and the increasing
number of available white women,
Negro women were to a very large
extent displaced. Wages for domestic
service for the rank and file have
fallen in the past twelve months
from $10.00 a week without any
laundry work to $7 and $8 with
laundry work.... The numbers
driven into domestic work are very
large."

62. A good description of this
conflict is in J. Stanley Lemons, *The
Woman Citizen: Social Feminism in
the 1920s* (Urbana: University of
Illinois Press, 1973), chap. 7 and
passim.

63. Mary Van Kleeck to Mary
Anderson, 21 February 1923, Van
Kleeck papers, unsorted, Sophia
Smith Collection, Smith College,
Northampton, Mass.

64. In one notable instance where
the law adversely affected a group of
New York City women printers, the
women were able to get an
exception made for their occupation.

65. See, for example, Judith A.
Baer, *The Chains of Protection: The
Judicial Response to Women's Labor*

Legislation (Westport, Conn.: Greenwood Press, 1978), especially chap. 6.

66. Chairman Pitzer of the National Association of Corporate Schools, Fifth Annual Convention, Addresses, Reports, Bibliographies, and Discussions, 1917, p. 105.

67. Quoted in Margery Davies, "A Woman's Place is at the Typewriter," in Richard Edwards et al., eds., *Labor Market Segmentation* (Lexington, Mass.: D.C. Heath, 1975), p. 290.

68. Harry Braverman, *Labor and Monopoly Capital: The Degradation of Work in the Twentieth Century* (New York: Monthly Review Press, 1974), p. 305.

69. Ibid., p. 321.

70. Quoted in Lois Garvey, "The Movement for Vocational Education, 1900–1917: An Analysis of Its Consequences for Women" (M.A. thesis, Sarah Lawrence College, 1976), p. 36.

Four: Women's Social Mission

1. Quoted in Nancy Cott, ed., *Root of Bitterness: Documents of the Social History of American Women* (New York: E.P. Dutton & Co., 1972), p. 147.

2. Ibid., p. 144. See chap. 3 of this book for additional examples.

3. Edward T. James and Janet Wilson James, eds., *Notable American Women* (Cambridge, Mass.: The Belknap Press of Harvard University Press, 1971) is a good beginning point for the study of these women.

4. William Ladd, *On the Duty of Females to promote the Cause of Peace* (1836; reprint ed., New York: Garland Publishing, 1971), p. 42.

5. Gerda Lerner, *The Grimké Sisters from South Carolina* (New York: Schocken Books, 1967), p. 187.

6. Barbara Berg, *The Remembered Gate: Origins of American Feminism* (New York: Oxford University Press, 1978), chap. 8.

7. Ibid., pp. 183, 187.

8. Thorstein Veblen, *The Theory of the Leisure Class* (1898; reprint ed., New York: Viking Compass, 1967), p. 342.

9. Carroll Smith-Rosenberg, "Hysterical Women: Sex Roles and Role Conflict in Nineteenth Century America," *Social Research* 39 (Winter 1972): 652–78; and Charlotte Perkins Gilman, *The Yellow Wallpaper* (Old Westbury, N.Y.: Feminist Press, 1973).

10. Mary Roth Walsh, *Doctors Wanted: No Women Need Apply: Sexual Barriers in the Medical Profession, 1835–1975* (New Haven, Conn.: Yale University Press, 1977).

11. Charlotte Perkins Gilman, *The Home, Its Work and Influence* (1903; reprint ed., Urbana, Ill.: University of Illinois Press, 1972), p. xxi.

12. Sheila Rothman, *Woman's Proper Place: A History of Changing Ideals and Practices, 1870 to the Present* (New York: Basic Books, 1978), pp. 65–66.

13. Gerda Lerner, "The Community Leadership of Black Women: The Neighborhood Union of Atlanta, GA," in *The Majority Finds Its Past* (New York: Oxford University Press, 1979).

14. For a description and analysis of social Darwinist thought see Richard Hofstadter, *Social Darwinism in American Thought* (Boston: Beacon Press, 1955).

15. Rothman, *Woman's Proper Place*, pp. 73–74.

16. Mary Ryan, *Womanhood in America from Colonial Times to the Present* (New York: New Viewpoints, 1975), p. 211; and Rothman, *Woman's Proper Place*, p. 67.

17. Allen Davis, *American Heroine: The Life and Legend of Jane Addams* (New York: Oxford University Press, 1973), p. 64. See also Davis' comprehensive book on the settlement movement as a whole, *Spearheads for Reform* (New York: Oxford University Press, 1967).

18. Blanche Wiesen Cook, *Female Support Networks and Political Activism: Lillian Wald, Crystal Eastman, Emma Goldman* (New York: Out and Out Press, 1979), offers a good example of such support networks.

19. Davis, *American Heroine*, pp. 205, 207.

20. Louis Brandeis, *Decision of the United States Supreme Court in Curt Muller vs. State of Oregon and Brief for the State of Oregon* (New York: National Consumers League, 1908), p. 6.

21. Elizabeth Kemper Adams, *Women Professional Workers* (Chautauqua, N.Y.: Chautauqua Press, 1921), pp. 9, 12, 15, 3.

22. Ibid., pp. 73, 74, 65, 186.

23. See Susan Cayleff, "The Eradication of Female Midwifery" (M.A. thesis, Sarah Lawrence College, 1978). For data on the numbers of professional workers see Janet Hooks, *Women's Occupations through Seven Decades*, U.S. Department of Labor, Women's Bureau Bulletin #218 (Washington, D.C.: Government Printing Office, 1947), pp. 65–66.

24. From an unidentified newspaper clipping, 23 March 1923, Bureau of Vocational Information Archives, box 4, file 23, Schlesinger Library of Radcliffe College, Cambridge, Mass.

25. *The Nation*, 6 July 1927, p. 10.

26. "Trying to be Modern," *The Nation*, 17 August 1927, p. 155, reprinted in Elaine Showalter, ed., *These Modern Women* (Old Westbury, N.Y.: Feminist Press, 1978).

27. Data on married women workers can be found in Joseph Hill, *Women in Gainful Occupations: 1870–1920*, Census Monographs #9 (Washington, D.C.: Government Printing Office, 1929), chap. 9; and James A. Sweet, *Women in the Labor Force* (New York: Seminar Press, 1973). Since the census often undercounts women, these data should be used cautiously. For recent data see *Employment in Perspective: Working Women*, issued quarterly by the U.S. Department of Labor, Bureau of Labor Statistics. These figures are from Report 565, first quarter, 1979.

28. Ruth Milkman, "Women's Work and the Economic Crisis: Some Lessons from the Great Depression," *Review of Radical Political Economics* 8 (Spring 1976):82; and Margaret Jarman Hagood, *Mothers of the South: Portraiture of the White Tenant Farm Woman* (1939; reprint ed., New York: Norton, 1977), p. 175.

29. Ferdinand Lundberg and Marynia F. Farnham, *Modern Woman: The Lost Sex* (New York: Harper and Brothers, 1947), p. 201.

30. Ibid., 360, 370.

31. Helen Z. Lopata, *Occupation: Housewife* (New York: Oxford University Press, 1971) p. 96, 98.

32. Doris B. Gold, "Women and Voluntarism," in Vivian Gornick and Barbara Moran, eds., *Woman in Sexist Society* (New York: New American Library, 1971), p. 533–34.

33. James T. Patterson, "Mary Dewson and the American Minimum Wage Movement," *Labor History* 5 (Spring 1964).

34. Herta Loeser, *Women, Work and Volunteering* (Boston: Beacon Press, 1974), introduction.

35. Veblen, *Theory of the Leisure Class*, p. 171.

36. Quoted in W. Elliot Brownlee and Mary M. Brownlee, *Women in the American Economy: A Documentary History, 1675-1929* (New Haven, Conn.: Yale University Press, 1976), pp. 337, 339.

37. Robert Sklar, ed., *The Plastic Age: 1917-1930* (New York: George Braziller, 1970), pp. 94-95.

38. Betty Friedan, *The Feminine Mystique* (New York: Dell Publishing Co., 1963).

39. Sara Evans, *Personal Politics: The Roots of Women's Liberation in the Civil Rights Movement and the New Left* (New York: Alfred A. Knopf, 1979).

Five: Changing the Shape of the Work Force

1. Edna McKnight, "Jobs—for Men Only? Shall We Send Women Workers Home?" *Outlook and Independent*, 2 September 1931, p. 18; Frank L. Hopkins, "Should Wives Work?" *The American Mercury* 39 (December 1936):409-416; and Jane Allen, "You May Have My Job: A Feminist Discovers Her Home," *Forum* 87 (April 1932): 228-231.

2. Ruth Milkman, "Women's Work and the Economic Crisis: Some Lessons from the Great Depression," *Review of Radical Political Economics* 8 (Spring 1976):73-97; Claire-Howe, "Return of the Lady," *New Outlook* 164 (October 1934):34-37; and Anna Spencer Garlin, "Should Married Women Work Outside the Home," *Eugenics* 4 (1931):21-25.

3. Claire-Howe, "Return of the Lady," p. 38.

4. Data on depression unemployment can be found in U.S. Department of Labor, Women's Bureau, Bulletins #113 and 159 as well as in Bulletin #218 which summarizes trends from 1880 to 1940. For some examples of data broken down to reflect the characteristics of the labor force by age, sex, number of children, etc., see "Varieties in Employment Trends of Male and Female Workers," *Monthly Labor Review* 31 (July 1930):19-28; and the 1940 Census of Populations, Volume III, p. 5.

5. Winifred Wandersee Bolin, "The Economics of Middle Income Family Life: Working Women During the Great Depression," *Journal of American History* 65 (June 1978):60-74; Milkman, "Women's Work and the Economic Crisis," pp. 81-85; Laetitia Conrad, "Some Effects of the Depression on Family Life," *Social Forces* 15 (1936):76-81; and Paul H. Douglas, "Some Recent Social Changes and their Effect Upon Family Life," *Journal of Home Economics* 25 (May 1933):361-370.

6. Janet Hooks, *Women's Occupations through Seven Decades*, U.S. Department of Labor, Women's Bureau Bulletin #218 (Washington, D.C.: Government Printing Office, 1947), pp. 126, 127, 132, 133.

7. *Fortune* 27 (February 1943):98-102 and ff. William Chafe, *The American Woman: Her Changing Social, Political and Economic Roles* (New York: Oxford University Press, 1972), chap. 6 has a good discussion of shifts in women's occupations during the war years.

8. Nell Giles, *Punch in Susie! A Woman's War Factory Diary* (New York: Harper and Brothers, 1943), p. 92.

9. Lucy Greenbaum, "The Women Who Need to Work," *New York Times Magazine*, 29 April 1945, p. 43.

10. Ibid., p. 16.

11. National Manpower Council, *Womanpower* (New York: Columbia

University Press, 1957), pp. 327, 328.

12. National Commission on Working Women, *Fact Sheet*, quoted in the *New York Times*, 23 September 1977, p. B2.

13. Karl Tauber and James A. Sweet, "Family and Work: The Social Life Cycle of Women," in Juanita M. Kreps, ed., *Women and the American Economy: A Look to the 1980s* (Englewood Cliffs, N.J.: Prentice Hall, 1976), pp. 67–68.

14. Jerry Flint, "Oversupply of Younger Workers is Expected to Tighten Jobs Race," *New York Times*, 25 June 1978, p. A1.

15. For a good summary of this legislation see Phyllis A. Wallace, "Impact of Equal Opportunity Laws," in Kreps, *Women and the American Economy*, pp. 123–145.

16. *New York Times*, 11 June 1978, p. F3.

17. *Spokeswoman*, 15 December 1978, p. 3.

18. *New York Times*, 10 December 1971, p. 20.

19. "Social Security and Sex Discrimination," *New York Times*, 1 March 1979, p. A18.

20. *Spokewoman*, 15 May 1978, p. 9.

21. Gary Becker, *The Economics of Discrimination* (Chicago: University of Chicago Press, 1957).

22. *City News*, 22 September 1978, p. 22.

23. Carol Stack, *All Our Kin: Strategies for Survival in a Black Community* (New York: Harper and Row, 1974).

24. "Women at Work," *Newsweek*, 6 December 1976, p. 76.

25. Juanita Kreps and Robert Clark, *Sex, Age and Work: The Changing Composition of the Labor Force* (Baltimore: Johns Hopkins University Press, 1975), pp. 79–82.

26. Carolyn Shaw Bell, "The Next Revolution," *Social Policy* 6 (October 1975):6.

Index

The numbers in italics indicate pages with photographs.

Photograph Acknowledgments

Cover: The National Archives. *Frontispiece:* Culver Pictures. *2-3:* Culver Pictures. *10:* William Wilson, Historic Mobile Preservation Society. *11:* Culver Pictures. *20-21:* Lewis Hine, Culver Pictures. *36, 37 (top):* Brown Brothers. *37 (bottom):* Frances Benjamin Johnston, Library of Congress. *54-55:* courtesy of A.T. & T. Company Photo Center. *78 (top):* F.P. Burke, The National Archives. *78-79 (bottom), 79 (top), 102-103:* Brown Brothers. *122:* Culver Pictures. *123 (top and bottom):* Brown Brothers. *136-137, 152 (top):* © by Bettye Lane. *152 (bottom):* Harry Wilks; Stock / Boston. *153:* © by Bettye Lane.

✓ 1. Issue of supplanting ♀ in labor force
by other, cheaper labor pools

✓ 2. Use p71 graph for provocation { race questⁿ
+ conditions

✓ 3. trapping women by
consumer image p132

4. consider age of labor force
✓ → " change of nature of work
→ " increasing age of population

5. How are women in vanguard mid. mngt
handling their jobs/careers as they approach
a significant block of high mngt.

6. Family stability wasn't good. Child abandonment
✓ was very high. Divorce is only part.
Family breakup data is much more
accurate and consistently high.
Much more chaotic than K-H. image

7. comparable worth

8. Dean: if not for wages then certainly in hono